The Canada-U.S. Automotive Agreement:

An Evaluation

by

Carl E. Beigie

CANADIAN-AMERICAN COMMITTEE
sponsored by
National Planning Association (U.S.A.)
Private Planning Association of Canada

Legal Deposit — 2nd Quarter 1970
Quebec National Library

Library of Congress Catalog Card Number: 75-119893

1970, $3.00

National Planning Association (Washington, D.C.) and
Private Planning Association of Canada (Montreal, Que.)

Printed in Canada

ii

STATEMENT
BY THE CANADIAN-AMERICAN COMMITTEE
ON *The Canada-U.S. Automotive Agreement: An Evaluation*
by Carl E. Beigie

Over its twelve-year life, the Committee has followed no event in Canadian-American relations with more sustained interest than the Automotive Agreement. The question of some form of special regime for this industry has been an active item at the Committee's semi-annual meetings since early 1964, when the first stirrings of disquiet over the unilateral Canadian "duty remission scheme" set the stage for negotiating the bilateral Agreement that was enacted the following year.

By and large, both Canadians and Americans welcomed the Agreement as a creative resolution of an awkward and threatening predicament, though, to be sure, uneasiness existed on both sides regarding specific conditions and its method of enactment. But in any event, it was the Agreement's actual effects that soon became the big issue, and an increasingly controversial one even after statistics on its operation began to emerge. Official data on bilateral automotive trade, a key indication of performance, came to diverge widely between the two countries. Furthermore, even where the numbers were clear, they gave rise to conflicting interpretations as to their significance for the parties involved and for the general welfare of both countries. Accordingly, the Canadian-American Committee, guided by a special subcommittee chaired by Mr. Franklin Lindsay, commissioned a thorough review of the Agreement, with special emphasis on its practical results to date and the issues thereby raised.

For this project the Committee was fortunate to obtain the services of Mr. Carl E. Beigie, then on the faculty of the University of Western Ontario and currently an international economist at the Irving Trust Company in New York. Mr. Beigie's analysis and conclusions are his own. Without necessarily endorsing them, the Canadian-American Committee recommends publication of his study in the belief that it makes a significant and timely contribution to the current appraisal of the Agreement in both countries.

MEMBERS OF THE CANADIAN-AMERICAN COMMITTEE SIGNING THE STATEMENT

Co-chairmen

ROBERT M. FOWLER
President, Canadian Pulp and
Paper Association

JOHN R. WHITE
Vice President and Director,
Standard Oil Company (New Jersey)

Members

T. N. BEAUPRÉ
Chairman of the Board and
President, Domtar Limited

J. A. BEIRNE
President, Communications Workers
of America, AFL-CIO

RUSSELL BELL
Director of Research, Canadian
Labour Congress

HAROLD BOESCHENSTEIN
Chairman, Executive Committee,
Owens-Corning Fiberglas Corp.

PHILIP BRIGGS
Vice President, Metropolitan Life

E. D. BROCKETT, JR.
Chairman of the Board,
Gulf Oil Corporation

EARL L. BUTZ
Vice President for Special Projects,
Purdue Research Foundation

FRANÇOIS E. CLEYN
Chairman of the Board and Chief Executive
Officer, Cleyn & Tinker, Ltd.

THOMAS E. COVEL
Vice President, Aluminium
Limited, Inc.

PAUL DESMARAIS
Chairman, Power Corporation of
Canada, Limited

WILLIAM DODGE
Secretary-Treasurer, Canadian
Labour Congress

A. D. DUNTON
President, Carleton University

H. E. EKBLOM
Senior Vice President,
The Chase Manhattan Bank

EDMUND H. FALLON
Senior Vice President and Chief Administrative
Officer, Agway Inc.

MARCEL FARIBAULT
Montreal, Quebec

A. J. FISHER
President, Fiberglas Canada Limited

HAROLD S. FOLEY
Vancouver, British Columbia

G. H. GALLAWAY
President, Crown Zellerbach
International

F. PEAVEY HEFFELFINGER
Honorary Chairman of the Board and Member
of the Executive Committee, Peavey Company

GILBERT W. HUMPHREY
Chairman, The Hanna Mining Company

CURTIS M. HUTCHINS
Chairman of the Board,
Dead River Company

R. A. IRWIN
President, Consolidated-Bathurst Ltd.

CRAWFORD T. JOHNSON
Assistant to the Chairman,
Baker Industries

VERNON E. JOHNSON
Calumet, Quebec

JOSEPH D. KEENAN
International Secretary, International
Brotherhood of Electrical Workers, AFL-CIO

WILLIAM LADYMAN
International Vice-President,
International Brotherhood of
Electrical Workers, AFL-CIO-CLC

iv

v

The Canada-U.S. Automotive Agreement:

An Evaluation

CONTENTS

TABLE OF CONTENTS *(continued)* PAGE

x

List of Tables

List of Charts

Introduction
and Summary of Conclusions

Introduction

On January 16, 1965, Canada and the United States signed an agreement concerning bilateral trade in automotive products. Given the ambiguous nature of this agreement, with formal and informal restraints contradicting in part the free trade implications of other provisions, it was perhaps inevitably destined to be viewed differently in the two countries. Even now, more than five years after the Automotive Agreement was signed, the two governments have not reached a complete understanding on what they agreed to do.

On the surface, the Agreement appears to be a sectoral free trade pact providing for the eventual elimination of barriers to North American trade in automotive products, and such has been the interpretation that the United States has always held. To be sure, an annex to the formal intergovernmental Agreement made free entry into Canada conditional on maintaining certain production floors there; and, more importantly, the Canadian government extracted commitments from the vehicle-producers (most of whom were subsidiaries of U.S. firms) in the form of "letters of undertaking" that were designed to protect and increase Canada's share of North American automotive production. But while the United States has seen these production commitments as only transitional, Canada appears to regard them as being required indefinitely in an Agreement interpreted to be primarily a means for both expanding its sector of the industry and making it more efficient. If a conflict should arise between Canadian and North American efficiency, according to this view, protection of Canada's production share would be the overriding consideration.

At the time the Automotive Agreement was signed, official predictions of its economic effects were made publicly on both sides of the border.

1

In brief, the contention was that benefits to Canada did not have to come at the expense of equal — or, indeed, any — losses to the United States. Furthermore, the United States would share the benefits of Canadian efficiency gains because the main vehicle-producers were subsidiaries of American parents. In any event, it was argued, the United States was certainly better off with the Automotive Agreement of 1965 than with more restrictive alternatives that Canada might have adopted unilaterally to achieve the same production objectives.

These public predictions were based on the assumption that the Agreement would not produce an appreciable decline in the traditionally large U.S. automotive trade surplus with Canada. Production commitments by the U.S. vehicle-producers in Canada were seen as precluding any marked increase in the U.S. surplus during the short run, but it was argued that the impact of these commitments could be met largely from normal growth in Canadian demand for automotive products and would not necessitate a noticeable decline in the absolute amount of U.S. net sales to Canada.

Statistics on bilateral trade during the operation of the Agreement differ widely — an explanation of these discrepancies will be attempted in this study — but there is no doubt that U.S. production has lost a very substantial portion of its traditional share of the Canadian automotive market and that this loss is far greater than can be explained by strict fulfillment of the various production commitments. These commitments had really been designed to prevent precisely the opposite problem of a declining Canadian share, considered at that time to be the main negative implication for Canada of unrestricted free trade in this industry.

The unpredicted change in production shares has raised a number of issues that should have been clarified when the Automotive Agreement was negotiated, but this was not done. Key decisions regarding the future of the Agreement are now being formulated, and it is therefore appropriate to re-examine all the important and complex issues that are involved.

Outline of the Study

The Automotive Agreement of 1965 was the culmination of a sequence of events beginning with the realization in Canada that the efficiency of its automotive industry was low by world standards because it was structured to serve a limited domestic market isolated by tariff barriers at home and abroad. Part I of this study, "Problems and Initial Responses," examines the Canadian automotive industry prior to the Agreement, with special emphasis on its degree of inefficiency in comparison to production in the United States. We then discuss unilateral initiatives by Canada to improve the prospects for its automotive industry.

One of these initiatives — the "duty-remission plan" of 1963 — was of fundamental importance because it was challenged as being in conflict with U.S. customs law. The Automotive Agreement was a bilateral effort to provide a constructive alternative to a situation that could have had wide-ranging negative repercussions on Canadian-American economic relations.

Part II, "The Automotive Agreement and Its Effects," opens by describing the Agreement itself and comparing it with the previous tariff structure and Canada's unilateral plans. A subsequent chapter explains the effects of the Agreement that were anticipated at the time it was launched. This is followed by a detailed analysis of its actual effects to date, which is divided into two chapters.

• The first deals with the results in terms of integration of the Canadian and U.S. sectors of the industry; these results are highlighted by the efficiency gains in Canada brought about through restructuring of Canadian production to supply the entire North American market and to take advantage of the marked economies of scale and specialization in the industry.

• The second deals with the results in terms of changes in the Canadian and U.S. shares of North American production; it is in terms of these results that the main discrepancies between predicted and actual effects are shown to have arisen.

This analysis (in Part II) indicates that the vehicle-producers have overfulfilled, by a wide margin, their production commitments contained in the formal Agreement and the accompanying letter of undertaking with the Canadian government. Part III, "Evaluation and Outlook," begins by examining, first, several possible explanations for this overfulfillment; then, the consequences of this overfulfillment; and, finally, the implications of possible future policy options.

A number of complex technical problems are involved in an analysis of the Automotive Agreement. Discussion of these problems is kept as brief as possible in the main body of this study, but more detailed accounts are contained in separate appendices gathered together in Part IV. Appendices A and B reproduce the text of the Automotive Agreement and a sample of the letters in which the vehicle-producers agreed to meet certain conditions placed upon them by the Canadian government. The reader is referred especially to Appendix E, dealing with the difficulties of reconciling automotive trade statistics in the two countries.

The Data: Scope and Limitations

One of the main data sources for this study is the annual *Report on the Operation of the Automotive Agreement* that the President of the

United States is required by law to present to Congress. The fourth *Report,* covering developments during 1969, will not be available until the late spring or early summer of 1970. Much of the data for 1969 can be obtained from other sources, although in some cases only part-year results had been released at the time this study was completed.

For a number of reasons, including problems of achieving comparability, it was decided to exclude all 1969 data and concentrate upon 1968, the last year for which a complete set of statistics was available. Preliminary indications are that 1969 showed a continuation of all trends reported in this study, strengthening the conclusions reached. The question of developments in the automotive trade balance is so important, however, that an exception was made by including data for the first nine months of 1969 (see Table 23, Chapter 8).

A major handicap experienced in this study was that available data often provide an insufficient basis for definitive conclusions. We make numerous suggestions regarding data deficiencies, but until these data are supplied, a deductive approach is required to come to grips with fundamental issues. The assumptions necessary to proceed with the analysis are spelled out as we go along.

Summary of Conclusions

Subject to the qualifications noted above, the main conclusions of this study can be summarized as follows:

• Efficiency in the Canadian automotive industry was substantially less than in the United States prior to the Agreement. Even though Canadian vehicle-producers imported a considerable amount of parts duty-free and paid wages that were about 30 percent lower than those paid to U.S. automotive workers, vehicle prices in Canada were markedly higher — on the order of 10 percent (after adjusting for the rate of exchange and net of sales taxes) — than in the United States. At the same time, the rate of return on capital employed in the two industries was, in the aggregate, about the same.

• This difference in efficiency levels was caused by the inability of Canadian automotive production to reap the advantages of economies of scale and specialization by producing an excessively diversified range of products for a small domestic market isolated by tariff barriers at home and abroad.

• Following the Agreement integration of the Canadian and U.S. sectors of the automotive industry proceeded quite rapidly. Two indications of its extent are that (a) imports from the United States accounted for more than 40 percent of the Canadian market for North American-produced vehicles in 1968, compared with under 3 percent in 1964, and (b) about 60 percent of all vehicles produced in Canada during 1968 were exported, compared with less than 7 percent in 1964.

• The vehicle-producers have exceeded the conditions required to achieve duty-free treatment in Canada by a substantial margin. On the basis of a rough calculation, we estimate an overfulfillment of about U.S.$396 million by 1968, although this probably overstates somewhat the leeway that was available to the producers. In any event, the over-fulfillment was large, and appears to have increased by an additional substantial amount during 1969. As a direct result of this overfulfillment, coinciding with less than expected growth in the Canadian domestic market, the U.S. automotive trade surplus with Canada has declined sharply whichever data are used, although it had been officially predicted at the time the Agreement was signed that this balance would not change significantly.

• The amount of the decline in net U.S. automotive sales to Canada is not accurately reflected in any of the reported measures of the trade balance. Our suggestion is to compute a balance for automotive parts, using the import statistics of both countries, and a balance for vehicles, using both countries' export statistics, and then combine them. On this basis the U.S. surplus declined from U.S.$586 million in 1964 to U.S.$229 million in 1968, a drop of U.S.$357 million.

• Efficiency in Canadian automotive production has increased sharply following the Agreement. This is reflected in the fact that although Canada has gained considerably in terms of its share of North American *production,* its share of North American automotive *employment* was about the same in 1968 as in 1964. On the basis of information that is available, it is impossible to tell for sure whether the improvement in Canadian efficiency has been sufficient to overcome the initial Canadian disadvantage.

• In the absence of direct evidence on comparative efficiency levels, an analysis of the Canadian vehicle-producers' overfulfillment of their production commitments is made. There are four possible explanations for the estimated overfulfillment: (1) inflation of the commitments as a result of Canada's valuation procedures for imported vehicles; (2) a desire by the manufacturers to maintain an adequate safety margin in their performance; (3) "lumpiness" in the addition of production facilities; (4) disappearance — and possible reversal — of Canada's initial relative production-cost disadvantage. Each of these factors was important, but the analysis of the reasons behind the overfulfillment suggests that the competitive positions of Canada and the United States in automotive production may have been significantly altered as a result of the Agreement. The inevitable lumpiness of new investment in assembly facilities, and hence in assembly operations, could have been compensated by a shift of parts production back to the United States, but was not.

• Even if part of the overfulfillment can be attributed to favourable — or at least not unfavourable — costs in Canada, it is important to recognize that decisions regarding the location of additional production facilities are based on comparative production *costs* and not comparative production *efficiency*. Throughout the period of the operation of the Agreement there has been a cost advantage to Canada in terms of wages paid to Canadian automotive workers.

• The Canadian-U.S. differential in vehicle prices has narrowed perceptibly since the Agreement, but a noticeable margin of about 4 percent remains. We are not able to conclude with certainty that the remaining price differential can or cannot be justified on the basis of differentials in costs, but the size of the price gap appears large considering the substantial overfulfillment of the vehicle-producers' commitments.

• Given the degree of integration in North American automotive production that has been achieved, the short-term behaviour of production shares will be determined by demand for the vehicle models in which Canada specializes. The pattern over the longer term will be determined on the basis of developments in two areas that cannot be predicted at this time. First, the question of production guarantees to Canada, currently the subject of intergovernmental review, will establish whether there will be a floor on Canada's share. Second, the major vehicle-producers have agreed to equalize, by September, 1970, the wages they pay in Canada and the United States, as expressed in the currencies of the respective countries. Until that time there will be a nominal wage advantage in Canada; and even then a real Canadian wage advantage in the amount of the exchange differential ($1 Can. = $0.925 U.S.) will remain. Furthermore, for many independent Canadian parts-producers there is not even a commitment to nominal wage parity at the present time. If this wage advantage more than compensates for any difference in labour productivity that might remain, a guaranteed floor on Canada's production share would be redundant, and the United States balance of automotive trade with Canada might just as easily be in deficit as in surplus during the years ahead.

• On balance, the Agreement may have produced a net economic loss to the United States. However, the amount of the decline in net U.S. automotive sales to Canada is a totally inaccurate measure of any loss involved; until the profit performance of the Canadian subsidiaries of U.S. parents is determined, there can be no conclusive proof that a net loss did indeed occur.

• A negative feature of the Automotive Agreement is that it was an *ad hoc* measure worked out to allay specific pressures, while questions of possible long-term complications — when asked — were rationalized away at the time. It was negotiated in secret and presented to the U.S. Congress, the Canadian Parliament, and the general public in both countries as a *fait accompli*. Complications and misunderstandings concerning the Agreement have arisen. This study concludes that their economic solution will require a long-term Canadian-American commitment to seek the kind of North American efficiency gains that the Agreement has demonstrated are possible in one sector through a program that would be more widely beneficial to both countries. The experience with the negotiation, implementation, and operation of the Automotive Agreement of 1965, however, may make public acceptance of such a commitment in the United States more difficult to achieve.

Part I:
PROBLEMS AND INITIAL RESPONSES

1

The Canadian Automotive Industry
Prior to the Agreement

The sequence of events that culminated in the Canada-U.S. Automotive Agreement of 1965 was provoked by one fundamental fact: the Canadian automotive industry was unable to compete effectively in international markets because of its traditional position as a high-cost duplication in miniature of the United States' automotive industry. Just why this was so will be discussed in detail in this chapter and the one that follows. But first, let us make a few comparisons between Canada and the United States.

In most respects differences between these two countries are less striking than differences between various regions within them. Both are large, well-endowed nations enjoying a very high standard of living. The crucial difference, one causing many others, is that Canada's population is only about one-tenth that of the United States.

Table 1 presents several economic indicators for the two countries in 1964, the year just prior to the Automotive Agreement. Canada's small population and its lower level of per capita income combined to produce a total market for goods and services (GNP) which was only about 7 percent of that in the United States. With a lower per capita disposable income in Canada — 67 percent of the U.S. level — we might expect that Canadians would not be able to spend as great a portion of their incomes on durable goods. Table 1 confirms that this was the case in 1964.

A. The Automobile in Canadian Life

It is rather surprising that the level of motor vehicle ownership in Canada shown in Table 1 was so high in 1964, particularly in view of generally higher prices there than in the United States. In large part this reflects the fact that in both countries the automobile has become a necessity for most people.

Canadian consumers have preferences that are generally similar to those of Americans in terms of the type of automobile they buy. Canadians do tend to buy relatively more overseas-manufactured (i.e., European and, more recently, Japanese) cars, but as Table 2 and Chart 1 show, the differential has narrowed significantly in the past several years. The similarity in the trends of overseas import purchases that appear in Chart 1 is also interesting. During the late 1950s such imports surged in both countries, followed by a sharp decline in the early 1960s as compacts were introduced by North American producers. By 1964 the impact of the compacts had largely worn off, and imports of overseas-manufactured automobiles began to rise again. But whereas in 1968 the United States had surpassed the previous peak rate in imports established during 1959, Canada was importing at a rate equal to about half the 1960 peak.

TABLE 1

COMPARISON OF SELECTED ECONOMIC INDICATORS,
CANADA AND THE UNITED STATES, 1964

	Canada	United States	Canada as a % of United States
Population ('000)	19,235	192,120	10.0
Gross national product (bil. $ U.S.)	$ 43.8	$631.7	6.9
Per capita magnitudes (rounded to nearest U.S. $10):			
Gross national product	$2,280	$3,290	69
Personal income	$1,690	$2,580	66
Disposable income	$1,530	$2,270	67
Personal consumption:	$1,430	$2,090	68
Durables	$ 170	$ 310	55
Non-durables	$ 690	$ 930	74
Services	$ 560	$ 850	66
Total motor vehicles ('000)	6,225	86,297	7.2
Motor vehicles per person	.32	.45	71

Note: Exchange rate used in the above calculations: $1 Can. = $0.925 U.S.

Sources: Dominion Bureau of Statistics, *National Accounts, Income and Expenditures,* Cat. No. 13-201, annual.

U.S. Department of Commerce, Office of Business Economics, *The National Income and Product Accounts of the United States, 1929-1965: Statistical Tables.*

Motor Vehicle Manufacturers' Association, *Facts and Figures of the Automotive Industry,* 1966.

TABLE 2

OVERSEAS IMPORTS AS A PERCENTAGE OF NEW CAR SALES,
CANADA AND THE UNITED STATES, 1955-68

Calendar Year	Canada (1)	United States (2)	(1) − (2)
1955	5.7	0.8	4.9
1956	8.4	1.6	6.8
1957	12.9	3.5	9.4
1958	20.5	8.1	12.4
1959	26.8	10.2	16.6
1960	28.1	7.6	20.5
1961	23.1	6.5	16.6
1962	15.0	4.9	10.1
1963	9.2	5.1	4.1
1964	10.7	6.0	4.7
1965	10.6	6.1	4.5
1966	9.8	7.3	2.5
1967	10.9	9.3	1.6
1968	14.1	10.5	3.6

Note: Imports exclude vehicle trade between the two countries. U.S. sales are based on new car registrations.

Sources: Computed from data compiled by Dominion Bureau of Statistics, *New Motor Vehicle Sales,* Cat. No. 63-208, annual, and R. L. Polk & Co.

In the past six years, then, automobiles produced by U.S. vehicle-manufacturers or their Canadian subsidiaries have accounted for almost 90 percent of total sales in Canada. Each model of such automobiles is essentially the same, whether produced in Canada or the United States.[1] It is difficult to explain just why Canadians have the tastes in cars they do, but constant exposure to American advertising and other cultural influences undoubtedly acts to maintain the basic similarity between Canadian and American preferences. On the other hand, the pattern of development of the motor vehicle industry in Canada and the nature of competition within it may have been equally important factors, ones that should be kept in mind when considering the 1965 Agreement.

B. The Basic Nature of the Canadian Automotive Industry

American subsidiaries play a major role in many Canadian industries, but there are few cases in which the degree of dominance has been as total as in motor vehicles.[2] The only producers of any real size are subsidiaries of the "Big Three" (Chrysler, Ford, and General Motors), a situation that

---

[1] A small percentage of Canadian production and sales is accounted for by subsidiaries of overseas firms operating assembly plants in Canada (see footnote 3 below).
[2] See A. E. Safarian, *Foreign Ownership of Canadian Industry* (Toronto: McGraw-Hill, 1966), Chap. 1.

Chart 1

OVERSEAS IMPORTS AS A PERCENTAGE OF NEW CAR SALES

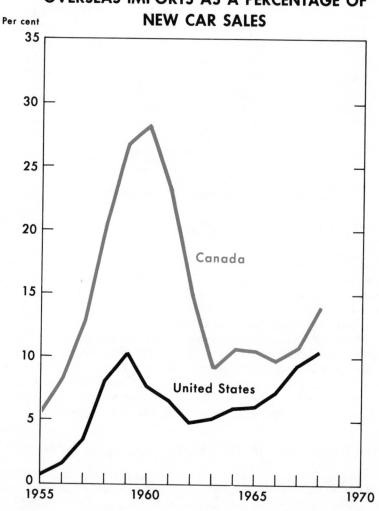

Source: Table 2

has been more or less true since the 1920s.[3] Prior to the signing of the Agreement these subsidiaries concentrated operations in the assembly of vehicles from parts sub-assemblies imported from the United States, although Canada's content requirements contributed to the growth of a domestic parts-supplying industry. The reason for these developments is to be found both in the nature of scale economies in the industry and in the type of restrictions the two countries imposed on automotive trade between them.

1. Scale of Production

The production of a completed motor vehicle involves a multitude of components and processes. While the complexity of the industry makes it difficult to generalize, for most stages of production there are significant advantages in attaining large volumes. As a rough indicator of the magnitudes involved, Professor Joe Bain has estimated that an integrated firm producing less than 300,000 passenger cars per year would face a major cost handicap, and continuing reductions in unit costs could be realized for outputs ranging up to about 600,000 cars per year.[4] (The 600,000 figure, incidentally, is almost exactly the level of total new car sales in Canada during the 1964 model year — August 1, 1963, to July 31, 1964 — just prior to the first impact of the 1965 Agreement.) The advantages of size are particularly important in the production of major components such as engines and in the stamping of auto bodies, but much less so in assembly, where Bain estimates that 60,000 to 180,000 vehicles per year exhaust scale economies.

Economies in the production of a single model are by no means the only advantages of large size in this industry. The evolution of the American automobile industry may not be based entirely on efficiency grounds, but the clear fact is that there is a trend in all producing countries towards larger and fewer manufacturers of vehicles. Even though scale economies do change over time and depend upon a number of factors, there is little doubt that these economies have been so great that, bearing in mind the size of the Canadian market, an independent domestic manufacturer producing a vehicle right from scratch would have had to concentrate on very few lines to achieve any degree of operating efficiency.

---

[3]The "Big Three" acounted for roughly 90 percent of Canadian production in 1964. As in the United States, American Motors barely continues to maintain its existence in Canada. In 1966, Studebaker was forced to abandon vehicle production after trying to salvage operations by moving all car production to Canada. The Agreement had little, if any, bearing on Studebaker's disappearance. Meanwhile, stimulated by various incentives, two European firms have recently begun to assemble in Canada — Volvo in Nova Scotia and Renault-Peugeot in Quebec. Assembly in Sydney, Nova Scotia, of the Japanese Toyota is just getting under way.
[4]Joe 'S. Bain, *Barriers to New Competition* (Cambridge: Harvard University Press, 1956), pp. 244-46.

Whether the Canadian consumer would have accepted the resultant limitation of options — even for a totally Canadian product — is a moot point, but there are good reasons for the doubts that have been expressed on this score.

2. Protection of Canadian Automotive Production

Nominal Protection: Canadian Tariff Rates. The pattern of automotive production that has taken place in Canada over the years reflects the impact of tariff policies. One of the original attractions to American firms of production in Canada was the tariff advantage Canada received in certain countries as a result of its membership in the British Commonwealth. After the Second World War, however, foreign markets for North American vehicles diminished quite markedly, so Commonwealth preferences were no longer of much practical significance. What remained an important influence right up to the time of the 1965 Agreement was Canada's own tariffs on vehicle and parts imports from the United States.

Canada's basic tariff policy affecting automotive imports was established in 1936. The rates in effect prior to the Agreement are shown in Table 3.[5] As far as imports of completed motor vehicles were concerned, the tariff was simple enough — 17.5 percent. In the case of parts, however, the policy was quite complex, with several different rates and conditions in effect. For a long list covering most parts (line 2-A, Table 3), a tariff rate of 17.5 percent applied. There was no way of avoiding this tariff on parts that were of a class or kind made in Canada (line 2-A-i). For parts that were not of a class or kind made in Canada, the basic tariff rate was still 17.5 percent (line 2-A-ii-a), but duty-free import could be gained provided that the manufacturer attained a specified level of "Canadian content" in his vehicle production in Canada (line 2-A-ii-b).[6] Specifically, to qualify for duty-free entry of these parts the vehicle-producer had to show payments for Canadian parts and manufacturing costs amounting to 60 percent of the factory cost of passenger cars and 50 percent of the factory cost of commercial vehicles produced in Canada.[7] Finally, a tariff

---

[5]The rates shown were those under the most-favoured-nation (MFN) tariff. The rate under the British preferential tariff was uniformly zero. Beginning in October, 1962, Canada instituted a duty-remission plan which enabled producer-importers to recoup the duties they incurred by expanding certain categories of automotive exports. The basic tariff schedule remained unchanged, however. See Chapter 3 for a discussion of this remission program and its more comprehensive sequel.

[6]Actually, the requirement was that the content provisions be met from sources within the Commonwealth, but overseas sourcing had been negligible.

[7]This requirement applied to firms producing more than 20,000 cars a year in Canada. Firms producing less than 10,000 cars a year faced a content requirement of 40 percent, and firms producing between 10,000 and 20,000 cars a year had a 50 percent requirement. As of 1962, the "Big Three" and American Motors were each producing at least 20,000 cars a year. For commercial vehicles the 50 percent requirement was applied to firms producing more than 10,000 units. Firms producing less than 10,000 units faced a 40 percent content requirement. Chrysler did not reach the 10,000-unit level until 1964.

TABLE 3

AUTOMOTIVE TARIFFS, CANADA AND THE UNITED STATES, 1964

	Canadian Tariff	U.S. Tariff
1. Completed vehicles	17.5%	
A) Passenger cars		6.5%
B) Trucks		8.5%[a]
C) Buses		7.5%
2. Parts		8.5% (generally)
A) Specified parts:		
i) when of a class or kind manufactured in Canada	17.5%	
ii) when of a class or kind not manufactured in Canada		
a) and manufacturer does not meet content requirements	17.5%	
b) and manufacturer meets content requirements	Free	
B) All other parts (including, for example, passenger-car engines and brake linings)	25.0%	

[a]As a result of the "chicken war" with the European Economic Community, trucks valued in excess of $1,000 were dutied at a "temporary" rate of 25 percent.

rate of 25 percent was charged on imports of parts (line 2-B) that were not included in the main list, regardless of whether they were made in Canada or not and regardless of the amount of Canadian content achieved by the producer-importer.[8] Included in this category were such major items as brake linings, passenger-car engines, and, although the duty was not actually collected before October, 1962, automatic transmissions.

As for U.S. automotive tariffs, prior to the Agreement those covering completed vehicles and most parts ranged between 6.5 and 8.5 percent. While these rates were lower than the corresponding Canadian duty rates, they had a significant impact on the development of the Canadian industry, for reasons to be discussed shortly.

Real Protection: Content Requirements. The tariff rate structure in Canada presented vehicle-producers with a number of possible options.[9] A simplified example will show that the content provisions afforded a

8One special exception was a 7.5 percent tariff on heavy truck engines.
9On this point see Paul Wonnacott, "Canadian Automotive Protection: Content Provisions, The Bladen Plan, and Recent Tariff Changes," *Canadian Journal of Economics and Political Science,* February 1965, pp. 98-116; H. G. Johnson, "The Bladen Plan for Increased Protection of the Canadian Automotive Industry," *ibid.,* May, 1963, pp. 212-38.

degree of real protection to Canadian automotive operations that far exceeded the nominal tariff rate.[10] Suppose a U.S. vehicle-manufacturer charges U.S.$2,000 for a car sold in the United States. If he were to export the same car to Canada and receive the equivalent dollar amount for it, he would have to charge U.S.$2,350 owing to the 17.5 percent Canadian tariff. On the other hand, he might produce the car in Canada and sell it there for the same price of U.S.$2,350. In that case, assuming a 60 percent content requirement, he could import up to U.S.$940 — 40 percent of $2,350 — in duty-free parts towards the production of that car.[11]

For local assembly to be attractive, it is necessary only that the manufacturer be able to obtain domestically the remaining parts and services (including assembly costs) required to complete the vehicle at a cost of less than U.S.$1,410 ($2,350 minus $940). These same parts and services would have cost $1,060 in the United States ($2,000 minus $940), so the rate by which Canadian costs exceed U.S. costs is really just over 33 percent.[12] Because of the fact that low-volume assembly and production of some parts is reasonably efficient, the degree to which the cost of parts and services needed to fill out the residual content requirements could exceed costs in the United States might be even greater than this 33 percent average.[13,14]

Effects of the U.S. Tariff. The degree of real protection in the Canadian automotive tariff structure provided an inducement to assembly operations in Canada and stimulated domestic parts production to take advantage of the provisions in the content requirements. This is an example of how a country can structure its tariff policies so as to counteract the disincentives of a relatively small home market. But this counteraction was achieved at the expense of efficient production. An alternative course that Canada might have taken, one which would have brought fuller realization of scale economies, was for Canadian producers to concentrate

---

[10]We are interested here only in the effects of a tariff rate that is conditional upon the degree of domestic content achieved. Even if content performance does not affect tariff charges, there will still be a difference between the nominal and "effective" tariff rates if the tariff on a completed vehicle differs from the tariff on components or on materials used in producing the completed vehicle.

[11]Actually, the content requirement applied to factory cost, which was lower than sales value. Therefore, allowable imports would be lower in the example. While this gives an upward bias to the estimate of real protection, we have neglected this for the sake of simplicity.

[12]$(1,410 - 1,060) \div 1,060 = 0.33$.

[13]From this example it should be obvious that, with a given nominal tariff rate, the real rate of protection will be greater, the lower the domestic-content percentage required.

[14]Producers will not necessarily price Canadian-assembled vehicles at the same level as completed-vehicle imports — that is, U.S.$2,350 in the example. The real rate of protection may be more than is needed to warrant Canadian assembly, thus providing leeway for prices lower than those of comparable duty-paid imports.

on only a limited range of automotive products, relying upon export sales to achieve the necessary volume for efficient operations. This course, however, would have required access to the U.S. market. U.S. automotive tariffs, although relatively low (see again Table 3), were high enough to prevent Canadian production from competing effectively in that market.

The development of the Canadian automotive industry prior to the 1965 Agreement, then, was determined as much by tariffs that Canada could not control — those in the United States — as by those tariffs that Canada itself had established. In addition, as the Canadian market grew over time, another potential for cost reductions from higher volumes was largely dissipated as competition in the industry took the form of offering the consumer virtually the full range of models available in the United States. This proliferation of models in the domestic market, combined with the difficulty of establishing export markets, left little room for high-volume specialization in Canadian automotive production.

2

The Question of Inefficiency
in Canadian Automotive Production

The discussion to this point explains how the Canadian and the U.S. tariff and the Canadian content provision might have combined to permit automotive production to take place in Canada even if the level of efficiency there were much below that prevailing in the United States. But proving that inefficiency might exist does not tell us that it did exist or, if it did, to what degree. The question of the extent of inefficiency in Canadian production plays an important role in understanding the rationale for the 1965 Agreement and in evaluating the benefits to be gained from its implementation. It is imperative, therefore, that an attempt be made to answer this question, even though data are insufficient to be rigorously precise. In this section the available evidence is examined to see whether it supports the hypothesis of significant inefficiency in the Canadian automotive industry under the old tariff structure.

A. Price Comparisons

One type of evidence which is often cited as a sign of comparative production costs is the differential between vehicle prices in the two countries. While the exact difference has varied among models and over time, prior to the Agreement prices ranged between 10 and 17.5 percent higher for models produced and sold in Canada (after adjusting for

21

exchange-rate differences).[1] In a perfectly competitive industry this difference could be explained only on the basis of comparative costs. In an industry as concentrated as the motor vehicle industry, however, there is no necessary connection between price differences and cost differences; demand elasticities and the type of conduct followed by members of the industry must also be considered. The fact that price competition is anathema to oligopolists provides an explanation for the proliferation of Canada-assembled models — stimulating the Canadian consumers' taste for variety — and while this proliferation undoubtedly restricted efficiency gains over time, we have no way of knowing the extent for sure.

B. Export Performance

The very low level of automotive exports from Canada might also be taken as evidence of Canadian inefficiency.[2] This again, however, is misleading. Except for the Commonwealth countries' demand for North American vehicles, the United States presented the main potential export market for the type of automotive products produced in Canada.[3] But given the U.S. tariff, Canadian production costs would have to have been lower than those in the United States in order to compete in that market.

C. Manufacturing Performance

This leaves us with a set of statistics that relate to productivity performance in the two countries. It should be stressed that the lack of detail and comprehensiveness in these statistics is a serious handicap, and considerable caution must be exercised in interpreting them. Nonetheless, these are the only statistics that are now publicly available, and in most cases the differences are great enough to support general conclusions.

---

[1] See Ronald J. Wonnacott and Paul Wonnacott, *Free Trade Between the United States and Canada* (Cambridge: Harvard University Press, 1967), pp. 227-30. One would expect that the prices of vehicles sold in Canada should have been no higher than the U.S. price plus the tariff, after adjustment for exchange differences. But in 1964 a differential of 30.4 percent was quoted for the factory price of one model which was sold but not produced in Canada. See *Second Annual Report of the President to the Congress on the Operation of the Automobile Products Act of 1965* (Washington: Government Printing Office, 1968), p. 42. Here we have a case in which the Canadian tariff did not protect or induce production of the model in Canada, and evidently price elasticity of demand for this particular vehicle was thought to be so low and the nuisance of having to go to the United States to buy it so high that the company selling the car found price discrimination profitable and feasible.

[2] In 1961, for example, prior to the duty-remission schemes which are discussed in Chapter 3, Canada imported Can.$527 million and exported only Can.$43 million in automotive products.

[3] In non-Commonwealth countries, Canada and the United States faced the same MFN tariff rates. Since the automotive products made in Canada were virtually the same as in the United States, even a slight cost disadvantage would largely preclude Canada as a supplier to these markets.

Table 4 presents estimates of value of shipments, value added, production employees and their payroll, and the number of production man-hours for the automotive industries of the United States and Canada in 1963. This year was chosen because it is the latest for which a *United States Census of Manufactures* is available (another census was conducted during 1967, but the results were not available for this study) and because 1963 was fairly representative so far as the industry was concerned.[4] "Value of shipments" (line 1) corresponds to the value of sales at the factory and excludes taxes on the final product. "Value added" (line 2) is a measure of the contribution of factors employed within a plant to the final value of the product and is derived by deducting the cost of purchased materials and electricity and fuels consumed from the value of shipments. "Production workers" (line 3) rather than all employees are used because of differences in the reporting of non-production workers in the two countries.

Three technical points in Table 4 should be discussed briefly. First, we are, of course, dealing with two different currencies, and some standard for comparison must be adopted. No single standard is best suited for all purposes, but the method of converting Canadian values into U.S. dollars at the prevailing exchange rate has been used because it was felt that biases were thereby minimized. Second, the statistical reporting method differs between the countries in terms of product breakdown. Therefore, it is necessary to group statistics into two very broad categories: motor vehicles and parts; truck and bus bodies and truck trailers.

The third point is most critical to our analysis. As discussed above, automotive prices were generally higher in Canada during this period because of the degree of tariff protection. As a result, shipments and value-added amounts per employee will be inflated relative to those in the United States. The effects of this factor will be explained as we proceed with the analysis.

In Table 5, from the data in Table 4, nine ratios are derived and compared for similar product categories in the two countries.

1) VS/Emp: Column 1: Value of shipments per production worker is the crudest measure of productivity. As shown, the Canadian worker produced shipments, on average, equal in value to only about two-thirds of what an American worker produced in 1963. A weakness in using value of shipments, however, is that differences may arise simply because of variation in the degree of integrated activity and thus be totally unrelated to true differences in productivity. One would expect

---

[4]The two duty-remission programs in Canada, mentioned earlier and described in Chapter 3, did have some impact on the Canadian performance during 1963. The bias this introduces is slight, however, and in the direction of overstating Canadian productivity under the tariff structure that existed previously.

TABLE 4

AUTOMOTIVE MANUFACTURING STATISTICS, CANADA AND THE UNITED STATES, 1963[a]

United States	Motor Vehicles and Parts	Truck and Bus Bodies	Truck Trailers	Total	% of North American Total[b]
1. Value of shipments ('000)	$36,181,007	$476,733	$515,661	$37,173,401	95.0
2. Value added ('000)	$12,345,630	$229,472	$205,475	$12,780,577	94.7
3. Production workers	535,842	19,729	15,455	571,026	92.7
4. Production man-hours ('000)	1,192,606	40,897	30,896	1,264,399	92.6
5. Production payroll ('000)	$ 3,889,636	$ 98,359	$ 81,703	$ 4,069,698	94.6

Canada	Motor Vehicle Manufactures	Truck Bodies and Trailer Manufactures	Parts and Accessories Mfrs.	Total	% of North American Total[b]
1. Value of shipments ('000)	$ 1,402,575	$ 59,885	$504,004	$ 1,966,464	5.0
2. Value added ('000)	$ 455,218	$ 23,201	$230,562	$ 708,981	5.3
3. Production workers	21,543	2,979	20,266	44,788	7.3
4. Production man-hours ('000)	50,851	6,124	43,928	100,903	7.4
5. Production payroll ('000)	$ 126,809	$ 10,815	$ 95,653	$ 233,277	5.4

[a]All values are expressed in terms of U.S. dollars (using the exchange rate $1 Can. = $0.925 U.S.).
[b]North American total is the sum for Canada and the United States. Using figures from Table 1, Canada recorded the following shares of the North American totals in 1964: population — 9.1%; gross national product — 6.5%; total motor vehicles owned — 6.7%.

Source: See Table 5.

TABLE 5

Ratios in Automotive Industries, Canada and the United States, 1963[a]

	VS/Emp. (1)	VA/VS (2)	VA/Emp. (3)	MH/Emp. (4)	VA/MH (5)	Pay/Emp. (6)	Pay/MH (7)	VA/Pay (8)	(VA-Pay/Emp.) (9)
United States									
Motor vehicles and parts	$67,522	.341	$23,040	2,226	$10.35	$7,259	$3.26	3.17	$15,781
Truck and bus bodies and truck trailers	$28,206	.438	$12,362	2,041	$ 6.06	$5,118	$2.51	2.42	$ 7,244
Aggregate	$65,099	.344	$22,382	2,214	$10.11	$7,127	$3.22	3.14	$15,255
Canada									
Motor vehicles and parts	$45,602	.360	$16,403	2,267	$ 7.24	$5,321	$2.35	3.08	$11,082
Truck and bus bodies and truck trailers	$20,102	.387	$ 7,788	2,056	$ 3.79	$3,630	$1.77	2.15	$ 4,158
Aggregate	$43,906	.361	$15,830	2,253	$ 7.03	$5,208	$2.31	3.04	$10,621
Canada/United States Ratios									
Motor vehicles and parts	0.68	1.06	0.71	1.02	0.70	0.73	0.72	0.97	0.70
Truck and bus bodies and truck trailers	0.71	0.88	0.63	1.01	0.63	0.71	0.71	0.89	0.57
Aggregate	0.68	1.05	0.71	1.02	0.70	0.73	0.72	0.97	0.70

[a]In this table employment and payroll refer to production workers only. All values are expressed in terms of U.S. dollars (using the exchange rate $1 Can. = $0.925 U.S.).

Glossary: VS = Value of Shipments
VA = Value Added = VS minus the cost of purchased materials (see footnote 5)
Emp = Number of Production Workers
MH = Production Worker Man-Hours
Pay = Production Worker Payroll

Sources: U.S. Bureau of the Census, *Census of Manufactures, 1963*, Vol. II, Part 2, *Industry Statistics* (Washington: U.S. Government Printing Office, 1966).
Dominion Bureau of Statistics, *Manufacturing Industries of Canada*, Section A, 1964, Cat. No. 31-203 (Ottawa: Queen's Printer, 1967).

differences in integration in the North American automotive industry because of the traditional concentration on assembly in Canada.

2) A common measure of the extent of integration is provided by the ratio of value added to value of shipments (VA/VS: column 2): a high degree of integration would produce a ratio approaching one; as one moves towards simple assembly, the ratio becomes lower, approaching zero as a limit.[5] Rather surprisingly, Table 5 seems to suggest a slightly higher degree of integration in Canadian automotive activity. This result is undoubtedly spurious.[6]

3) Because of this statistical relationship, Canadian productivity is somewhat higher in comparison with that in the United States when measured in terms of value added per production worker (VA/Emp: column 3) than in terms of value of shipments as in column 1.

4) In 1963, Canadian production workers spent more hours on the job than Americans (MH/Emp: column 4).

5) Adjusting for this difference in hours worked (VA/MH: column 5), we find that Canadian automotive workers accounted for 69 percent as much value added per hour during 1963 as their American counterparts. This figure provides a very rough measure for comparing productivity in terms of a single factor input, labour.

With detailed estimates of the capital stock employed in automotive plants in the two countries, it would be possible to carry this analysis further to consider differences in total factor productivity. Meaningful capital-stock estimates are not available, so another approach has been adopted.[7]

---

[5]Value added (VA) is, by definition, equal to value of shipments (VS) minus the cost of purchased materials (CM). That is, $VA = VS - CM$. In a nearly-self-contained operation, few materials are bought, and VA and VS are nearly equal. Therefore, the ratio of VA to VS is close to one. As CM increases, the ratio falls.
[6]Suppose the factory cost of a car is U.S.$1,000 in the United States and U.S.$1,100 in Canada. In the U.S. plant, U.S.$600 in materials are purchased, whereas U.S.$660 in purchases are made by the Canadian plant. The ratio of VA to VS will be the same in both countries, 40 percent. If Canadian purchases represent duty-free imports, however, a greater percentage of the physical components of the car have been brought in by the Canadian plant, indicating lower real integration despite the same level being shown in nominal terms. In other words, the higher VA to VS ratio (column 2) in Canada may have been simply a reflection of higher-cost automotive activity there.
[7]There are really two problems that arise in trying to estimate the capital input. The first is a lack of publicly available information in Canada. Only Ford of Canada publishes an annual report, and in this report there is consolidation of activities in Canada, Australia, New Zealand, South Africa, and Singapore. Second, even when information is available, as in the United States, the figures are on a consolidated basis that is too gross for our purposes.

The burden of higher production costs or lower efficiency in the Canadian automotive industry might be borne by three separate groups: consumers through higher prices; workers through lower wages; shareholders through a lower rate of return on their capital. The impact of higher product prices has already been reflected in the value-added figures. Therefore, we now turn to the question of the burden on factors of production — labour and capital.

6) In 1963, Canadian automotive workers earned a little over 70 percent as much as American workers, in terms of U.S. dollars, whether measured annually (Pay/Emp: column 6) or on an hourly basis (Pay/MH: column 7). It is interesting to note, by way of a brief digression, that this wage differential nearly matched the differential in value added per worker. As a result, the value added received for each dollar paid in wages (VA/Pay: column 8) was about the same in both countries.

7) The next step is to subtract wages per production worker from value added per production worker [(VA - Pay)/Emp: column 9]. The result is equal to R/Emp, where R is the return to all factors employed by a firm other than production workers. These factors consist mainly of non-production employees and various types of capital equipment. Table 6 provides us with estimates of the number of non-production employees and their salaries, along with various ratios of interest. From Table 6 we see that Canada employed considerably more non-production workers per production employee than did the United States (column 4).[8] The average level of salaries paid to non-production employees in Canada was 68 percent of that in the United States (column 3), and the non-production workers' wage bill per production employee was about 17 percent greater in Canada (column 5).

8) Subtracting all wages and salaries from manufacturing value added (Table 6, column 6), we find that on a per-production-worker basis, Canada produced at a level only 63 percent of that in the United States. The measure "value added minus total wages," with some minor adjustments, equals the return to capital employed by the firm. This return can be written as K times r, where K is the value of the capital stock and r is the rate of return.

---

[8]A difference in the classification of non-production workers contributes to the higher ratio in Canada. More important, however, automotive manufacturers have confirmed that Canadian subsidiaries were run as separate firms, with extensive duplication of administrative staffs. The 1965 Automotive Agreement has led to integrated production, but there is a continuing need to maintain, for example, separate legal and customs departments. The salaries of these administrative personnel can be spread over a greater volume of production in the United States than in Canada because of differences in market size.

TABLE 6

Non-Production Employees in Automotive Industries, Canada and the United States, 1963[a]

	Number (1)	Salaries ('000) (2)	Salaries per Non-Prod. Emp. (3)	Non-Prod. Emp. per Prod. Emp. (4)	Non-Prod. Sal. per Prod. Emp. (5)	VA minus Wages & Sal. per Prod. Emp. (6)
United States						
Motor vehicles and parts	114,084	$1,057,635	$9,271	.213	$1,974	$13,807
Truck and bus bodies and truck trailers	8,711	$ 66,114	$7,590	.248	$1,879	$ 5,365
Aggregate	122,795	$1,123,749	$9,151	.215	$1,968	$13,287
Canada						
Motor vehicles and parts	15,359	$ 97,467	$6,346	.367	$2,331	$ 8,751
Truck and bus bodies and truck trailers	1,150	$ 5,683	$4,942	.386	$1,908	$ 2,250
Aggregate	16,509	$ 103,150	$6,248	.369	$2,303	$ 8,318
Canada/United States Ratios						
Motor vehicles and parts	0.135	0.092	0.68	1.72	1.18	0.63
Truck and bus bodies and truck trailers	0.132	0.086	0.65	1.56	1.02	0.42
Aggregate	0.134	0.092	0.68	1.72	1.17	0.63

[a]All values are expressed in terms of U.S. dollars (using the exchange rate $1 Can. = $0.925 U.S.).

Source: See Table 5.

9)   As we have mentioned above, it is extremely difficult to obtain estimates of the capital stock employed in automotive plants in Canada and the United States. On the basis of a very rough exercise, however, we can show that the value of capital employed per production worker may have been sufficiently low in Canada so that r, the rate of return on that capital expressed in U.S. dollars, was very nearly the same in both Canada and the United States.[9] In other words, the burden of inefficiency in Canadian automotive production under the old tariff structure may not have been borne to any significant degree by owners of capital, although it is possible that the availability of better statistics would prove otherwise.[10]

D. Comparisons of Automotive Activities at the Regional Level

Table 7 computes the various ratios shown in Tables 5 and 6 for each of the census regions in the United States in 1963. Canada's results are also reproduced for comparison. Considerable variation occurs among U.S. regions, as is consistent with the fact that some areas specialize in assembly. But comparing these results with those for Canada, we find that Canada generally ranked at or near the bottom in terms of most measures.

Two points in this table are worth mentioning specifically. First, Canada led by a considerable margin in terms of the ratio of non-production employees per production worker (line 12), suggesting a costly duplication of staff. Second, the total return to capital per production worker (line 14) in Canada was much lower than for any region of the United States except in the insignificant automotive sector of the Mountain area — this despite the fact that in some U.S. regions wage rates (line 8) were not that much higher than in Canada.

The picture that emerges from this analysis is that the Canadian automotive industry had no parallel in any of the regions of the United States during 1963. Yet in terms of size, the Canadian operations were on a par with regions other than the main producing centre of the East North Central district (Michigan, Ohio, Indiana, Illinois, and Wisconsin). This tends to confirm further the argument that Canada's automotive tariff structure prior to the 1965 Agreement had produced an industry that was a costly, excessively diversified miniature of the U.S. industry.

---

[9]See Technical Note in Appendix C. Because of the similar rates of corporate taxation in Canada and the United States, we have disregarded the distinction between before- and after-tax returns.
[10]This tentative conclusion is based on the average performance for a number of firms. Even if the conclusion is in fact valid, it is quite possible that some firms earned a rate significantly higher in Canada than in the United States, while others earned a rate significantly lower.

TABLE 7

REGIONAL AUTOMOTIVE ACTIVITIES IN NORTH AMERICA, 1963

(Figures reflect the ratio of a region's performance in comparison with the average U.S. performance in the combined automotive industries.)

	New England	Middle Atlantic	East North Central	West North Central	South Atlantic	East South Central	West South Central	Mountain	Pacific	All Canada
1. VA[c]	0.010	0.097	0.676	0.070	0.059	0.022	0.017	0.001	0.049	0.055
2. Emp.[a,c]	0.011	0.100	0.721	0.048	0.042	0.018	0.015	0.002	0.042	0.078
3. VS/Emp.[a]	0.91	0.99	0.88	1.77	1.71	0.99	1.16	0.37	1.50	0.67
4. VA/VS	0.99	0.97	1.06	0.82	0.82	1.22	0.97	1.40	0.77	1.05
5. VA/Emp.[a]	0.89	0.96	0.94	1.45	1.40	1.21	1.12	0.52	1.16	0.71
6. MH/Emp.[a]	0.98	1.00	0.99	1.04	1.07	0.99	1.06	0.89	1.00	1.02
7. Pay/Emp.[a]	0.80	1.00	1.02	0.99	0.98	0.71	0.83	0.67	0.97	0.73
8. Pay[a]/MH	0.81	0.96	1.02	0.95	0.92	0.72	0.79	0.76	0.97	0.72
9. VA/Pay[a]	1.12	0.94	0.92	1.46	1.43	1.70	1.35	0.77	1.19	0.97
10. (VA-Pay[a])/Emp.[a]	0.94	0.97	0.90	1.66	1.60	1.44	1.25	0.44	1.25	0.70
11. Pay[b]/NPW[b]	0.92	1.14	1.02	1.02	1.00	0.86	0.93	0.83	0.95	0.68
12. NPW[b]/Emp.[a]	1.21	1.11	0.95	1.04	1.07	1.07	1.03	1.34	1.24	1.72
13. Pay[b]/Emp.[a]	1.11	0.92	0.97	1.06	1.06	0.91	0.95	1.11	1.18	1.17
14. (VA-All Wages)/Emp.[a]	0.91		0.89	1.75	1.68	1.52	1.30	0.34	1.26	0.63

[a]Refers to production employees only.

[b]Refers to non-production employees only.

[c]Expressed as a ratio to total for the United States.

Source: Derived from U.S. Bureau of the Census, *Census of Manufactures, 1963*, Vol. II, Part 2, *Industry Statistics* (Washington: U.S. Government Printing Office, 1966).

E. Summary of Chapters 1 and 2

The development of the Canadian automotive industry prior to the Automotive Agreement reflected the interaction of three forces:

1) Canada's automotive tariff policy, in terms of both basic tariff rates and the content provisions, encouraged assembly operations and some parts production in Canada.

2) The U.S. automotive tariff effectively foreclosed the main export market for Canadian automotive products, thereby restricting the options for high-volume specialization.

3) Rivalry among manufacturers led to a proliferation of models produced in Canada. This diversification of production limited the opportunities to realize efficiency gains from domestic market growth.

As a result of this pattern of development, the Canadian segment of the North American vehicle industry suffered a substantial handicap in terms of production efficiency. The degree of inefficiency is reflected by the following facts:

1) Motor vehicle prices were at least 10 percent higher in Canada.

2) Employees were paid about 30 percent less in Canada than in the United States.

3) The return to capital was probably no higher, on average, in Canada than in the United States.

From the challenges of this situation arose Canadian responses which came first in the form of unilateral steps to improve the competitive stance of the Canadian automotive industry.

3

Unilateral Canadian Initiatives

The 1965 Automotive Agreement did not just happen overnight, nor was it an isolated act of invention. Rather, it grew directly from a series of unilateral attempts by Canada to amend the structure of its automotive industry. Any evaluation of the Agreement must be made against the background of these prior efforts.

A. Basic Canadian Concerns

At the outset, it is important to consider certain preoccupations that influenced the formation of Canada's economic policies during the late 1950s and early 1960s.

Being a small nation in terms of population, Canada had always relied heavily upon trade to maintain its high standard of living. Merchandise imports equaled roughly one-sixth of Canada's GNP, and there was little doubt that the demand for foreign goods would grow at least as rapidly as GNP. In light of this, it is understandable that Canada should have been concerned with assuring a steadily increasing flow of receipts from foreign countries to finance these imports.

Canada was concerned about the form as well as the amount of its foreign-exchange receipts. Traditionally, current-account deficits had been offset by long-term capital flows into Canada. But capital inflows gave rise to interest and dividend outflows in the future, and there was always the possibility of net amortization. In 1957, the net burden of interest and dividend payments on Canada's current account was Can.$435 million, or one-third the level of net long-term capital inflows that year, which were Can.$1,320 million. After 1957, net long-term capital inflows fell off;

they stood at only Can.$637 million in 1963. That same year, the net interest and dividend payments burden, which had continued to grow, reached Can.$630 million, or about the same as net long-term capital inflows.[1] If this trend continued, Canada would have to put greater emphasis upon increasing its exports of goods more rapidly than its imports.

It was consistent with Canada's rank among the advanced economies of the world that it should attempt to improve its merchandise trade position so there could be a gradual reduction in its reliance upon net capital inflows as a means for achieving balance of payments equilibrium. But about this time two additional developments came to the surface which signaled to the Canadian government that economic evolution might have to be given a push.[2]

First, a considerable proportion of the capital that had come to Canada had been in the form of U.S. direct investment, particularly for the financing of the Canadian activities of American subsidiaries and the acquisition of Canadian-owned firms. There had always been disquiet among some over the degree of U.S. ownership of Canadian industry, but in 1956 this disquiet became more widespread and intense with the report of the "Gordon Commission."[3]

Second, even if Canada had not been concerned with the form of capital inflows from the United States, there was reason for growing uncertainty about the amounts of these inflows that might be available in the years ahead. Increasing pressures on the international payments position of the United States were developing, and these pressures eventually led to programs aimed at limiting outflows of U.S. capital, beginning with the Interest Equalization Tax in 1963. Canada felt it should have been given an exemption from these capital-restraint programs almost as a matter of course, given its traditional large current-account deficits with the United

[1]Dominion Bureau of Statistics, *The Canadian Balance of International Payments* (Ottawa: Queen's Printer, various years).
[2]The potential implications for Canada of both these developments extended well beyond the narrow question of how the merchandise trade balance might have to adjust to take account of them. Still, to the extent that the trade balance could be improved, there would be an increase in the flexibility of Canada's policy options. For a more complete discussion of the linkages between the Canadian and the U.S. capital markets, see Robert Dunn and Thomas L. Powrie, *The Canadian-American Financial Relationship* (Montreal and Washington: Canadian-American Committee, forthcoming).
[3]*Royal Commission on Canada's Economic Prospects: Preliminary Report* (Ottawa: Queen's Printer, 1956). This commission was headed by Walter L. Gordon, who, in June, 1963, as Finance Minister, introduced a budget creating special tax benefits for companies meeting certain requirements with respect to Canadian ownership and resident directors. For a different view on the problem see A. E. Safarian, *The Performance of Foreign-Owned Firms in Canada* (Montreal and Washington: Canadian-American Committee, 1969).

States. Exemptions were eventually granted, as it turned out, but the initiative had to come from the Canadian side.[4]

Finally, in addition to these other concerns, Canada was anxious to improve its merchandise exports as a means for attaining a different emphasis in its production activity. The feeling was that, while reliance upon primary industries might have been necessary in the past, Canada's future economic strength required that greater stress be placed upon secondary manufacturing. In part this desire arose from a belief that the terms of trade would continue to move against primary products and from a suspicion that foreign ownership of Canada's resources had been exploitive in the sense that additional processing of these resources prior to export would enable Canada to recoup higher profit margins. But probably the single most important reason for seeking to expand secondary manufacturing exports was the growing concern that Canada's population of only twenty million provided a market that was much too small in terms of the requirements for efficiency in modern industrial activity. Only by producing for much larger markets, it was widely believed, could Canada continue to assure a rising standard of living for its rapidly growing labour force.

Against the background of these basic Canadian concerns, it is obvious why, during the late 1950s, automotive production was singled out for special investigation. The surge of imports of European vehicles just then (Table 2 and Chart 1) was highlighting the deteriorating role of this secondary industry in Canada's over-all position on the current account of its international balance of payments. As shown in Table 8, prior to World War II Canada had been a net importer of automotive parts but a substantial exporter of vehicles. After the war, Canada's exports of vehicles fell off rapidly, while vehicle imports rose steadily. By 1960, Canada was importing 162,000 vehicles more than it was exporting. At the same time, parts imports rose in line with domestic production, yielding a net import position of over Can.$290 million in 1960. The total deficit on automotive-products trade in 1960 was Can.$528 million, with these products representing 10.5 percent of all merchandise imports but only 0.1 percent of all merchandise exports.

B. Efforts to Aid the Automotive Industry

1. The Royal Commission Proposals of 1961

In August, 1960, the Canadian government appointed Dean Vincent W. Bladen as a one-man royal commission charged with scrutinizing the

---

[4]An example of the potential impact on Canada of U.S. capital-restraints programs was seen in early 1968. On January 1, President Johnson announced harsh measures further limiting U.S. capital outflows. Soon thereafter, the Canadian dollar underwent severe pressure in foreign exchange markets, until an exemption for Canada was fully worked out in March, 1968.

TABLE 8

BALANCE ON CANADA'S AUTOMOTIVE TRADE WITH THE WORLD:
1921-50 BY FIVE-YEAR ANNUAL AVERAGES, 1951-68 ANNUALLY

	Cars (number)	Commercial Vehicles (number)	Parts ($'000 Can.)
1921-25 annual average	30,949	8,013	− 11,020
1926-30 annual average	16,882	18,483	− 32,256
1931-35 annual average	19,782	7,304	− 14,301
1936-40 annual average	22,499	25,618	− 26,524
1941-45 annual average	2,751	143,383	32,641
1946-50 annual average	− 10,886	20,698	− 95,547
1951	− 5,450	15,488	− 190,221
1952	7,001	31,092	− 185,444
1953	− 25,202	10,368	− 227,859
1954	− 31,188	− 2,991	− 177,619
1955	− 36,613	− 4,912	− 252,451
1956	− 62,078	− 10,126	− 294,640
1957	− 54,552	− 6,958	− 270,101
1958	− 90,786	− 8,004	− 248,695
1959	− 144,171	− 12,261	− 290,229
1960	− 153,469	− 8,471	− 290,176
1961	− 97,370	− 9,359	− 314,238
1962	− 82,781	− 4,805	− 429,509
1963	− 44,120	807	− 515,719
1964	− 54,213	8,781	− 567,301
1965	− 58,617	16,684	− 686,572
1966	882	90,043	− 721,709
1967	28,712	161,121	− 805,789
1968	85,159	214,783	− 1,032,798

Source: Dominion Bureau of Statistics, Cat. Nos. 65-004 and 65-007, as quoted in *Facts and Figures of the Automotive Industry* (Toronto: Motor Vehicle Manufacturers' Association (Canada), various issues).

nature and prospects of the Canadian automotive industry. After an intensive investigation, Bladen issued a report in April, 1961, recommending a number of changes in the ground rules for Canadian automotive production.[5] Although only one of his proposals was adopted — removal of the 7.5 percent excise tax on vehicle sales — Bladen's report was noteworthy for its "extended content" concept that laid the basic framework for subsequent action.

Bladen realized that the *raison d'être* for the existing Canadian automotive industry was import substitution, leaving it poorly structured for a good cost performance. This fact had once been disguised by Canada's tariff advantage in the Commonwealth, but developments after

[5]*Report of the Royal Commission on the Automobile Industry* (Ottawa: Queen's Printer, 1961).

World War II had removed even this source of demand. Canada was thus faced with two alternatives for improving the prospects for its automotive industry. On the one hand, its existing protection could be increased, but with the resulting fall in net imports probably would come a rise in domestic prices. Closer integration of Canadian production with that in the United States, on the other hand, could, with appropriate safeguards, reduce the dependence upon imports, while at the same time lowering domestic vehicle prices. To achieve the second alternative, Bladen proposed adopting an "extended content" plan.

Under Canada's then-existing tariff structure (Table 3), certain parts could be imported free of duty provided a Canadian "content requirement" were met: specifically, parts and services supplied in Canada had to equal 60 percent of the factory cost of a car.[6] But to count as Canadian content, parts and services had to be incorporated into cars that were assembled in Canada. Bladen's proposal was that Canadian content in automotive parts sold to foreign buyers (including affiliates of Canadian producers) should also be counted in determining Canadian content achieved. Thus the term "extended content." If a producer met the new content provisions, he could then import any vehicle and original part duty-free.[7]

Three additional features of the Bladen proposal should be noted:

• Replacement-parts production in Canada was favoured by being included as meeting content requirements through export, while its protection from import competition was maintained because duty-free treatment was not possible for these parts.

• All items imported as original equipment were given the same status. There was to be no special treatment for items such as engines and automatic transmissions (see Table 3).

• A car sold in Canada need not have even one dollar's worth of Canadian content. In fact, all cars sold in Canada could be imports made completely of foreign parts, and no duties would be due, just so long as exports of Canadian automotive products were sufficient to meet the "extended content" requirements.

---

[6]Strictly speaking, the requirement was in terms of Commonwealth content, but we will neglect the distinction in this discussion.

[7]Content requirements were to be revised to a sliding scale. For cars, the lowest rate was to be 30 percent on the first 5,000 either produced in Canada or imported by the firm under the "extended content" plan. The rate rose to a maximum of 75 percent on all cars in excess of 200,000 per year. For commercial vehicles the lowest rate was 30 percent on the first 5,000, and the highest rate was 60 percent on the excess over 50,000.

2. The Duty-Remission Plans

Rather than accept Bladen's recommendations, Canada set in motion two duty-remission plans — a pilot version in October, 1962, and a full version a year later — the second evoking sudden and serious controversy in the United States.

The *pilot plan* was launched on October 31, 1962. From that date the 25 percent duty on imports of automatic transmissions, previously suspended, was to be enforced and collected.[8] A manufacturer could recoup this duty, however, plus that on up to 10,000 engine-block imports (also duted at 25 percent), by increasing his exports of parts. Specifically, for every dollar of increased Canadian content in parts exports above the level attained during the base year (November 1, 1961, to October 31, 1962), duties would be remitted on a dollar's worth of automatic-transmission and engine-block imports.[9] It is important to note that there appears to have been no significant U.S. objection to the original Canadian move.

After one year of operation, this plan for duty rebates on transmissions and engines was broadened into the *full duty-remission program,* introduced on October 22, 1963.[10] This extended version allowed a manufacturer (defined as a firm producing in Canada at least 40 percent of the vehicles it sold there) to earn the remission of duties on one dollar's worth of *any* new vehicle and original parts imports for each dollar of Canadian content in vehicle and parts exports in excess of the November 1, 1961-October 31, 1962, base level.

By March, 1964, the full duty-remission plan threatened to become a critical issue in Canadian-American trade relations. The controversy arose from the plan's apparent conflict with the provisions of Section 303 of the U.S. Customs Act of 1930. This provided that if the U.S. Treasury Department determined that the export of a certain product reaching the United States was being subsidized by a "bounty or grant," a countervailing duty had to be imposed whether or not the import in question was causing domestic injury. During early 1964, administrative discretion held up such an investigation into the Canadian plan. But on April 15, 1964, the Modine Manufacturing Company of Racine, Wisconsin, filed a petition with the U.S. Bureau of Customs charging that the duty-remission plan constituted a subsidy within the meaning of the 1930 Customs Act.

---

[8]Order in Council P.C. 1962 — 1/1536, October 26, 1962.
[9]It will be recalled from Chapter 1 that, under the existing Canadian tariff structure (see Table 3), automatic transmissions and engines were included among those parts for which duties could not be avoided, regardless of the amount of Canadian content achieved.
[10]Order in Council P.C. 1963 — 1/1544.

The U.S. Treasury then began a process of formal review of the Modine petition. We have no way of knowing for certain what the final outcome of that review would have been, but an affirmative finding would have automatically brought a countervailing duty, nullifying what the Canadian government had hoped to achieve. Before any finding was reached, however, the Automotive Agreement was developed in a frenzy of bilateral negotiations taking place between April, 1964, and January, 1965. When this Agreement was signed by President Johnson and Prime Minister Pearson on January 16, 1965, the opinion in the matter of the Modine petition became academic.

C. Evaluation of the Canadian Plans

Before we turn in Chapter 4 to the Agreement itself, it is important to try to estimate what the effects might have been had either Bladen's "extended content" plan been enacted or the full duty-remission scheme remained in force for any length of time. Both these basic plans attempted to increase the effective market for Canadian automotive products by making removal of the tariff on imports conditional upon export performance.[11] In many other respects, however, the two approaches were quite different.

1. Replacement-Parts Production

Both plans would have had the same effect of granting a special incentive for replacement-parts production in Canada. A credit was to be given for the Canadian content achieved in replacement parts which were exported, but there was no way for a manufacturer to obtain duty-free treatment for Canadian replacement-parts imports. It would have been very difficult for Canada to administer a program that differentiated between original and replacement exports, but the difference in treatment between imports and exports would undoubtedly have played a role in any decision by the U.S. Treasury on the necessity for countervailing duties under the plans.

2. Barriers to the Rationalization of Production

A producer of automotive products for the North American market has a dual objective: production in the least-cost location and minimization of import duties. The question we seek to answer is how the two proposals might have altered existing barriers to the fulfillment of these two

---

[11]Even though only the full duty-remission plan of 1963 was challenged under the 1930 Customs Act in the United States, the same legal question would seem to be involved in the "extended content" and limited duty-remission plans. That question is whether making a country's tariffs on imports a function of export performance constitutes a subsidy triggering automatic U.S. sanctions.

objectives. It is on this point that the plans differed most, particularly in terms of mechanics.[12] Bladen's "extended content" plan would almost certainly have led to some increase in the efficiency of Canadian automotive production. Economies of scale could be realized more fully in production for all North America rather than for Canada alone, so some shifting of Canadian content from production for domestic sale to production for export markets would undoubtedly have taken place. Still, complete integration of the North American automotive market would have been blocked by the continuation of U.S. duties on imports from Canada.

The full duty-remission plan presents a more complex case. Cost reductions were possible in terms of shifting Canadian content from those parts which were protected by special duties.[13] But how much further shifting would there be? Here the firm faced a critical go, no-go decision. If it shifted Canadian content from vehicle production over to the production of parts, it would find that all imports became dutiable (although these duties could be recouped to the extent that parts exports were increased), whereas without the shift it could take advantage of the 60 percent content provision to import 40 percent of the factory cost of a car duty-free. The decision might have been made to go ahead and shift, but it would have been reached on the basis of tariff savings and *average* cost reductions, which could have involved significant increases in North American production costs for particular automotive products.

3. The Level of Canadian Production

The "extended content" plan would have required only a modest change in the value of Canadian automotive production in order to avoid the payment of Canadian duties by the firm.[14] There would have been a tendency for the real level of output to increase, however, as a result of any reduction in unit costs.

Again, the duty-remission plan is more difficult to analyze. Short of a decision by the firm to give up the 60 percent content in vehicles sold in Canada, some increase in production would have been required to attain the content needed to phase out production of specially-dutied items. This might have been all that happened. But if the firm did shift

---

[12]For an exhaustive study see Paul Wonnacott, "Canadian Automotive Protection...," *op. cit.*, pp. 98-116.

[13]To a firm which was producing so as not to pay any duties, the duty-remission plan produced a clear gain by enabling it for the first time to use Canadian content in other activities to offset high special duties (on engines, brake linings, etc.). See Table 3.

[14]The shift in the content schedule (see footnote 6 above) may have increased total output required. If factory costs were to fall in Canada as a result of either program, the value of required production, which was based on factory cost, would also have declined.

strategies and stopped meeting the 60 percent content requirement, it would have to match the increase in the Canadian content of its exports over the base-level period (November 1, 1961, to October 31, 1962) to the total value of Canadian automotive sales before it could avoid all Canadian duties. Therefore Canadian production would have to increase significantly.[15]

One might well ask whether Canadian automotive output would not have been expanded beyond the requirements for duty-free entry of all imports. The answer depends upon comparative costs. If, after all Canadian duties had been avoided, output could still be expanded at a cost that was lower than U.S. costs plus the U.S. tariff, production for export in Canada would indeed continue to rise, at least until this condition was no longer satisfied.[16] But again, the U.S. tariff would have remained a barrier to complete rationalization of North American automotive production with either of the Canadian plans.

4. Canada's Automotive Trade Balance with the United States

The effects of either plan on Canada's automotive trade balance with the United States can be deduced from their effects on the level of Canadian production. With a constant value of automotive sales in Canada, any increase in the value of Canadian production would lower its automotive trade deficit.

The Bladen plan would have had little immediate beneficial effect on the Canadian trade balance, and the potential deficit would have continued to grow by an amount equal to the marginal non-Canadian content ratio (i.e., one minus the Canadian content ratio) times the growth in the value of Canadian automotive sales.[17]

The full duty-remission plan, at a minimum, would have decreased the Canadian deficit somewhat. The most favourable outcome would have resulted if firms disregarded the 60 percent Canadian content in Canadian sales. In that event the balance would have ranged from the existing level

---

[15]Of course, the firm might also have changed its strategy regarding the payment of duties, in which case total Canadian production would have been within a band ranging from approximately 60 to 100 percent of the value of automotive sales in Canada.

[16]Additional production to replace U.S. imports would have taken place under both plans if Canadian costs were the same as, or lower than, U.S. costs. This option would be limited severely, however, by the need to produce small quantities, just as under the previous tariff structure.

[17]Note, however, that the highest marginal Canadian content requirement (75 percent for cars) was higher in the Bladen plan than the existing rate (60 percent for cars). This would have meant that the deficit would have grown by less — and Canadian production increased by more — under the Bladen proposal in comparison with existing policies.

to anywhere up to a small surplus equal to base-period (November 1, 1961, to October 31, 1962) exports, depending upon how much duty the firm was willing to pay.

5. Conclusions

Bladen's "extended content" plan and the full duty-remission program were both quite complex in their mechanics. It is doubtful whether anyone knew exactly what the final outcome of either plan would have been. Some gains in efficiency and marginally lower prices were reasonably certain.[18] The rest is pretty much speculation.

The critical question was one that received little attention at the time — comparative costs of Canadian and U.S. production under different tariff structures.[19] If Canadian costs could have been brought down enough through inducing production for export markets, the situation would have been favourable for Canada under either plan (assuming there was no violation of U.S. law against export subsidies). But the U.S. tariff level remained the critical problem. Unless costs in Canada could be reduced to a point sufficiently below U.S. costs to offset the U.S. tariff, the largest potential export market for Canadian automotive products was foreclosed except for those shipments needed to meet minimum content requirements for duty-free imports in Canadian operations. That was the way the matter stood, and there was nothing Canada could do on its own about the U.S. tariff.

---

[18]The decision to collect duties on automatic-transmission imports was the only major factor working in a contrary direction.

[19]What was essential was a study comparable in scope to Ronald J. Wonnacott and Paul Wonnacott, *Free Trade Between the United States and Canada, op. cit.*

Part II:

THE AUTOMOTIVE AGREEMENT AND ITS EFFECTS

4

The Automotive Agreement of 1965

Negotiations aimed at avoiding a potential economic confrontation over Canada's duty-remission plan took place in earnest during most of the second half of 1964. The result was the Automotive Agreement of 1965, a two-part plan establishing conditional duty-free trade between Canada and the United States in certain automotive products.

• Part one was a formal intergovernmental agreement (reproduced as Appendix A in Part IV of this study), which was signed by President Johnson and Prime Minister Pearson on January 16, 1965, and ratified by Congress in October, 1965.[1] This part of the plan was destined to continue in effect until and unless abrogated by either party.

• Part two — indispensable to the launching of part one — took the form of side conditions placed upon the vehicle-manufacturers by the Canadian government. These conditions were formalized in "letters of undertaking" transmitted from the manufacturers' Canadian subsidiaries to the Canadian government just three days prior to the signing of the intergovernmental Agreement. (A sample letter is reproduced as Appendix B in Part IV of this study.) The period during which these letters were to remain in force remains in some debate even now.[2]

To some extent the two parts of the 1965 Agreement were complementary, but not completely so. In the following sections the provisions of both parts will be discussed, followed in Chapter 5 by a review of their effects as anticipated at the time.

---

[1] Canada's participation in the plan was established by Orders in Council P.C. 1965 — 1/98, P.C. 1965 — 1/99, and P.C. 1965 — 1/100, all dated January 16, 1965.
[2] See Chapter 8.

A. The Formal Intergovernmental Agreement

The intergovernmental Agreement provided conditions for duty-free trade between the two countries in most new vehicles and parts to be used as original equipment. A number of specialty vehicles and chassis were excluded, as were all tires and tubes, whether for use as original or replacement equipment.[3] As is common in trade pacts of this general type, a provision was included to allow either party to abrogate the Agreement following a twelve-month notification period. In addition, it was stipulated that prior to the end of August, 1968, a joint review of the mechanics of the Agreement was to be completed by the two governments.[4]

1. U.S. Conditions

As far as the United States was concerned, the only further condition, contained in Article 3 of Annex B of the Agreement (see Appendix A) was that its imports from Canada must achieve a minimum North American content — after January 1, 1968, a uniform 50 percent — to earn duty-free treatment. This rule was aimed merely at preventing third-country producers, including those with limited North American production activity (presently Volvo, Renault-Peugeot, and Toyota) from using Canada as a channel for circumventing the U.S. tariff.

2. Canadian Conditions

Canada's conditions, listed in Annex A of the Agreement, were more significant because they were designed to influence the pattern of Canadian automotive production. The ˙primary condition [Article 2(5), Annex A] was that vehicle-manufacturers alone were able to achieve duty-free treatment, and in order to qualify as a "manufacturer," a firm had to satisfy requirements aimed at meeting two specific objectives of the Canadian government.

• The first objective was to assure continued growth in vehicle assembly in Canada. This was accomplished by specifying [Article 2(5) (ii) (A)] that for each class of vehicle (i.e., cars, trucks, and buses) the ratio of Canadian vehicle production to vehicle sales in Canada achieved by a "manufacturer" during each model year, expressed in net sales value,

---

[3]Tires and tubes mounted on a completed vehicle could be imported without duty.
[4]This review was completed without any recommendations for changing the Agreement being made. See the special report on this review by President Johnson on September 4, 1968, House of Representatives Doc. No. 379, 90th Congress, 2nd Session.

must be at least 75 percent *or* the percentage attained in the 1964 model year (August 1, 1963, to July 31, 1964), whichever was higher.[5]

• The second objective was to provide safeguards to independent Canadian parts-producers during the period of transitional adjustment to the effects of the Agreement. This was done through a requirement [Article 2(5) (ii) (B)] that the Canadian content (value added) in vehicles produced in Canada by a "manufacturer" must be no less than the absolute dollar amount achieved in the 1964 model year.

3. Treatment of Third Countries

The United States limited the duty-free treatment of automotive imports to trade with Canada, so U.S. participation in the Agreement technically violated the most-favoured-nation principle of the General Agreement on Tariffs and Trade (GATT). The United States applied for a waiver from GATT, which was granted on December 20, 1965. Canada, on the other hand, would allow any firm that could meet the qualifications set down for *bona fide* Canadian vehicle-manufacturers to import specified products duty-free from any country, so no breach of GATT rules was involved.

B. Commitments from the Manufacturers

The intergovernmental Agreement taken by itself gave the impression of being fairly close to a selective free trade pact. While there was definite protection of vehicle assembly in Canada, the Agreement contained no assurance whatsoever for growth in aggregate Canadian automotive production beyond the dollar amount achieved in the 1964 model year. The "letters of undertaking" between the producers and the Canadian government altered this impression strikingly. In these letters the producers agreed that by the end of the 1968 model year they would increase their value added in Canada by an amount equal to 60 percent of the growth in net sales value of cars and 50 percent of the growth in net sales value of commercial vehicles sold in Canada *plus* a total of Can.$260 million, divided as follows:

---

[5]Unlike the other conditions placed upon Canadian vehicle-manufacturers by the Agreement and the letters of undertaking, described below, this requirement carried no stipulation regarding the amount of Canadian value added. The key to fulfilling this ratio was in terms of final sales values only, and the number of vehicles and the intensity of assembly operations were not relevant except in relation to the need to meet other constraints. There are no publicly available statistics on the ratios achieved by individual producers in the 1964 model year, but we are reasonably certain that they were very close to 100 percent at that time for all major American subsidiaries (see, for example, Table 10, Chapter 6). The 75 percent floor was relevant primarily to smaller producers and those European or Japanese companies who, following the example of Volvo, might establish assembly operations in Canada.

TABLE 9

SUPPLEMENTARY COMMITMENTS BY AUTOMOTIVE PRODUCERS
IN THEIR "LETTERS OF UNDERTAKING"[6]

	Increase in Value Added in Canada Between the 1964 and 1968 Model Years	
	(mil. $ Can.)	(mil. $ U.S.)
General Motors	121.0	111.9
Ford	74.2	68.6
Chrysler	33.0	30.5
American Motors	11.2	10.4
Others	20.6	19.1
Total	260.0	240.5

We have said that the two parts of the Agreement — intergovernmental, and letters of undertaking — were somewhat complementary. The reason, as was discussed in Chapter 3, is that Canada was committed to protecting and strengthening its automotive industry. Without the assurances contained in the letters of undertaking, or something very similar, the Canadian government would not have signed the official agreement in its final form. Canada did sign, being convinced that once the Canadian automotive industry was integrated into a single North American industry, it would become efficient enough to motivate the U.S. parent manufacturers to give Canada its "fair share" of the continental production.[7] The letters of undertaking were extracted because the Canadian government feared that the U.S. producers might not be far-sighted enough to realize the potential efficiency of Canadian production or that, even if mindful of these advantages, they would prefer to play safe by serving the North American market from their home base.[8]

C. Comparison with Prior Tariff Structure and Alternative Plans

The 1965 Agreement accomplished the one thing the Canadians could not do by themselves: it eliminated U.S. tariffs on Canadian auto-

[6]Supplementary, that is, to their commitments to increase the value added in Canada by 60 percent of the growth in net sales value of cars and 50 percent of the net sales value of commercial vehicles sold in Canada.
[7]The term "fair share" has never been defined officially, but it has come to be accepted by some Canadians as meaning that Canadian production should closely approximate Candian purchases of automotive products. The results of the Agreement as judged by this criterion are the subject of Chapters 7 and 9.
[8]This later concern was probably provoked by some movement in the production of agricultural machinery from Canada to the United States in a situation where both countries allowed free entry and no restrictions were placed on the southward migration of manufacturing by U.S. and Canadian firms alike.

motive exports.[9] At the same time Canada, in order to stimulate efficiency in production, adopted a strategy which was basically a variation of Bladen's "extended content" plan. Manufacturers were still required to achieve specified levels of Canadian content, but a large part of that content could be met via production for export markets. In both these respects — removal of the U.S. tariff and greater provision for content fulfillment through exports — the Agreement was a positive step in the direction of removing the structural barriers to efficient production that had existed prior to the Agreement.

1. Potential Contributions to Efficiency

The formal Agreement required that a fixed *ratio* of Canadian vehicle production to vehicle sales in Canada be observed and that a fixed *value* of Canadian content in Canadian-produced vehicles be maintained. These conditions allowed for four types of rationalization that would bring forth efficiency gains in Canadian production.

1) Without increasing the production-to-sales ratio, the number of different models of vehicles produced in Canada could be reduced, with imports of discontinued models offset by exports of excess Canadian production of the limited range.

2) Without adjusting the mix between assembly and parts activity, a reduction in the number of vehicle models would allow for some specialization in the production of parts, although the number of kinds of parts produced could not be reduced immediately.

3) The amount of assembly activity could be increased, with a corresponding reduction in parts production.

4) As vehicle sales increased in Canada over time, further substitution of value added in assembly for value added in parts production would be possible.

Efficiency considerations arising from the letters of undertaking were quite different from those in the Agreement. Here the only requirements were for growth in Canadian automotive activity, growth which might take any form the producers desired — in production of vehicles or parts for the Canadian market, the U.S. market, or even third-country markets — conditional only upon an adequate progress report in terms of value added in Canada. As concerns that part of Canadian production growth which was tied to the growth of automotive sales in Canada, there was a clear efficiency gain in comparison with the old tariff structure. There, it will be recalled, Canadian content had to grow by the same amount — 60 percent of the net sales value of cars and 50 percent for commercial

---

[9]One alternative for achieving this effect unilaterally was never even attempted. Canada could have granted rebates or subsidies on exports to make up for the U.S. duties. There is no doubt that the United States would have invoked countervailing duties in this case.

vehicles — but the possibilities for specialization were much more limited. The part of Canadian production growth that was fixed at a predetermined level of Can.$260 million was a different matter. Unless Canadian costs were at least as low as U.S. costs, this requirement was a move away from efficient North American production.

2. Contrasts with Earlier Unilateral Proposals

The Agreement was markedly different from either the Bladen plan or the fully duty-remission plan in almost every detail except the provision to include all automotive production for export in the calculation of Canadian content achieved. A notable difference, of course, was that the Agreement excluded replacement parts entirely, whereas the other plans had granted special incentives for replacement-parts exports from Canada.

Another, and very important, difference was that the Agreement contained a rigid provision, the production-to-sales-ratio requirement, guaranteeing that assembly operations in Canada would grow in line with vehicle sales there. The Bladen plan provided no special incentive for Canadian assembly, and there was even a quirk in that plan that might have discouraged it.[10] An interesting incentive for assembly was contained in the full duty-remission plan, although it was indirect. The go, no-go decision the manufacturer was forced to make (Section C.2, Chapter 3) meant that he either continued assembly or else increased Canadian parts production sharply in order to avoid a significant increase in Canadian duties. This established that Canada was willing to give up its assembly activity, but only under very favourable circumstances. The Agreement opened new options and enabled Canada to protect assembly, while the letters of undertaking assured additional growth as well.

The novel feature of the letters of undertaking was that the Can.$260 million minimum growth requirement removed the uncertainty which would have existed if the full duty-remission plan had been continued. Given that Canadian content was guaranteed to grow in line with sales in Canada by one provision in the letters of undertaking, the removal of U.S. tariffs brought about by the Agreement assured Canada of at least as much benefit in terms of production and the automotive trade balance as it could have received with the duty-remission plan. The further commitment of $260 million production growth gave Canada a certain grant of something it could only have hoped to achieve with its previous program.[11]

[10]See Paul Wonnacott, "Canadian Automotive Protection . . .," *op. cit.,* pp. 107-08.
[11]Canadian production might have risen with duty remission in order to recoup duties on automatic transmissions even if the 60 percent content in Canadian sales was not abandoned. The amounts involved, however, would have been nowhere near Can.$260 million. The upward revision of the content rates that Bladen had proposed (footnote 6, Chapter 3) would have produced similar results to the fixed growth commitment. The timing would have been different, but eventually the figure of Can.$260 million would have been exceeded as vehicle sales in Canada continued to grow.

5

Anticipated Effects

Early in the bilateral negotiations that preceded the signing of the Agreement, it became clear that the highest levels of administration in the U.S. government attached great importance to a successful conclusion. U.S. officials realized that Canada was determined to do something about the poor prospects for its automotive industry. But the likelihood that Canada's latest remedial effort, the full duty-remission plan of 1963, would provoke automatic U.S. counteraction raised, as President Johnson later put it, "the prospects of a wasteful contest of stroke and counterstroke, harmful to both Canada and the United States, and helpful to neither."[1]

After the Agreement was signed early in 1965, considerable time was taken on the U.S. side in obtaining the implementing legislation from the U.S. Congress.[2] This delay reflected the unprecedented concern in two branches of government over the origin and the nature of the Agreement. In particular, the executive branch worried over departing from the traditional U.S. multilateral approach in trade matters, and this at an awkward time when the Kennedy Round of tariff negotiations was in

---

[1]Statement by President Johnson to U.S. Congress, House Committee on Ways and Means, *Hearings on H.R. 6960, United States-Canada Automotive Products Agreement,* 89th Congress, 1st Session, 1965, p. 6.

[2]The Agreement (Appendix A) was signed by President Johnson and Prime Minister Pearson at Johnson City, Texas, on January 16, 1965. Hearings on H.R. 9042, providing for U.S. implementation of the Agreement, were held by the House of Representatives on April 21-29, 1965, with the bill considered and passed by this body on August 31. The Senate held its hearings between September 14 and 21 and considered the bill on September 28-30, passing it on the latter date with amendment. On October 5 the Senate, and on October 8 the House, agreed to the conference report. Public Law 89-283, with the short title "Automotive Products Trade Act of 1965," was signed by the President on October 21, 1965.

progress. Meanwhile, the Congress resented being asked to ratify what it regarded as a *fait accompli,* in violation of what it considered to be its constitutional prerogatives in setting U.S. trade policy. It was displeased also with the letters of undertaking, in terms of both their contents and the method of procurement by Canada. While there were some advocates of the Agreement in the United States who saw positive benefits arising from it, others saw the main benefit in negative terms: preventing a trade war with a major economic and political ally. Some U.S. critics felt the whole affair suggested blackmail by Canada.

A. Economic Premises

The deliberate pace at which implementation in the United States proceeded also reflected considerable uncertainty over the economic consequences of the Agreement.[3] Proponents were convinced that while major gains would accrue to Canada, the United States would suffer little, if any, economic burden. Furthermore, they argued, the United States would certainly gain in a relative sense, since the impact of alternative courses for Canadian action would be much worse.[4]

There can be no argument with the assumption that positive over-all gains were possible from the Agreement. The then-existing inefficiency in Canadian automotive production could be greatly reduced by the removal

---

[3]Senator Vance Hartke of Indiana, a persistent critic of the Agreement, probably summarized the doubts best in the following remark:
> This started out as a rather humiliating thing for the United States to be faced with, in my opinion, but that is all right. We were threatened with unilateral action and then we went ahead and came in with this type of program [the Agreement]. But assuming that we forgive and forget what they did, they are going to have a larger percentage of the market and in addition a larger percentage of that market will be Canadian value added. The net result in my opinion can mean only one thing, a reduction in exports from the United States to Canada, and a reduction in jobs in the United States, unless the difference is made up by increased consumption beyond our normal growth pattern.

To which then-Secretary of Labor Willard Wirtz, an advocate for the Agreement, replied: "Reduction compared with what is our question or our difference." U.S. Senate, Committee on Finance, *Hearings on H.R. 9042, United States-Canadian Automobile Agreement,* 89th Congress, 1st Session (Washington: Government Printing Office, 1965), p. 343.

[4]It was suggested that in the absence of the Agreement Canada might follow the example of other countries — Australia, for instance — and sharply increase the Canadian content requirement from the existing 60 percent level for cars and 50 percent for commercial vehicles sold in Canada. Some U.S. critics argued that such a move would lead to a politically unacceptable increase in Canadian vehicle prices. While there is little point in engaging in speculation on what might have been, it should be noted that prices in Canada on major durable items such as electrical appliances are as much as twice the U.S. level. The willingness of Canadians to bear a higher price differential than that which already existed on motor vehicles is difficult to gauge, but the Canadian government might have found public support if other efforts on its part were frustrated by American counteraction.

of U.S. duties, enabling Canada to achieve the advantages of large-scale production for the entire North American market. Therefore, the proponents were correct in arguing that the Agreement was not a "zero-sum game" in which one country's gains must come at the expense of equal losses by the other side. It was possible for Canada to benefit from increased efficiency in production and still leave the United States in at least as favourable a position as before the Agreement was reached.

The economic case that was made in the United States also argued that it was unlikely that the Agreement would in fact lead to any marked disadvantage to U.S. interests. In addition to the assumption that positive gains were possible for both countries taken together, this argument rested on two further premises that no one questioned seriously at the time: (a) manufacturers would not significantly exceed the requirements of the Agreement and the letters of undertaking, and (b) Canadian automotive purchases would grow in line with recent experience. We will delay an evaluation of these premises until we have explored what has actually occurred during the life of the Agreement. In the remainder of this chapter we will review the anticipated effects of the Agreement in terms of both countries' interests, assuming these two premises, held to be valid by the Agreement's proponents, proved indeed to be so.

B. Potential Effects

Four different interest groups that might have been affected by the Agreement can be identified in each country: consumers of automotive products, producers of automotive products, employees in automotive industries, and the general public. It is true, of course, that a large number of individuals will belong to two or more of these groups, since automotive workers will usually be automotive consumers as well, and they may also be shareholders in various automotive manufacturing firms. Nevertheless, we will take up the case of each group separately and in turn.

1. Consumers

There was no reason to expect any adverse effect on consumers in either country as a result of the Agreement. In Canada, consumers could expect to receive at least some gain. It is true that the Agreement contained no guarantee that Canadian prices would fall relative to those in the United States. But the reduction in the costs of their Canadian operations would likely induce manufacturers to lower prices in order to realize greater sales in Canada. Whether the differential in prices could be eliminated is a question to which we will return in Chapters 9 and 10.

On the U.S. side, unless we believed that part of the cost burden of Canadian operations had been passed on to American consumers in the past, which is quite unlikely, no change in U.S. prices was to be expected from the Agreement.

2. Producers

Producers of automotive products can be divided into two groups: vehicle-producers and independent parts-manufacturers. With regard to vehicle-producers, the Agreement made sure that their interests would be served with the least possible inconvenience. Looked at realistically, this was probably the way it had to be, because the successful prosecution of the Agreement required the full cooperation of these firms. Accordingly, the Agreement allowed them to integrate their North American operations to a greater extent than had previously been possible; and in the process the pace of the reduction in relative Canadian prices was left to the producers' discretion, so that the inevitable transitional costs would be borne at least partially by the Canadian consumer.

In the case of the independent parts-manufacturers, the prospects were not so unambiguously positive. Taking the U.S. manufacturers first, the Agreement meant that any automotive part destined for new vehicles produced in Canada was now a possible item for export. Offsetting this promising prospect, however, was that of increased competition from Canadian producers. And because of the commitments in the letters of undertaking to expand Canadian production, this competition would not necessarily be based on the ability of U.S. producers to supply a part at the same or less cost than the Canadian firm. The Agreement meant, therefore, that while the U.S. independents could hope to gain a larger share of North American production of some parts, they were fairly certain to lose a portion of their share of others. While adjustments to such changes were always possible, the U.S. independents, unlike the U.S. vehicle-producers, were forced to bear virtually the full burden of adjustment themselves.[5]

The Canadian independents, it was supposed, started from a position of considerable inefficiency, so the task of adjusting to the Agreement would be greater for them than for the Americans.[6] Faced with the prospect of meeting American competition, it is understandable that some Canadian independents viewed the Agreement with hesitancy. But it did contain two provisions which should have eased their concern. First, while no individual firm was guaranteed protection, a continued rate of growth of total parts production was fairly well assured by the commitments in

---

[5]In both the United States and Canada, assistance was to be provided to firms and employees who had to make adjustments as a result of the implementation of the Agreement (see Chapter 9).

[6]For a thorough discussion of the problems facing the Canadian metal-stamping industry, see Henrik O. Helmers, *The United States-Canadian Automobile Agreement: A Study in Industrial Adjustment* (Ann Arbor: University of Michigan, 1967).

the letters of undertaking. Second, a transitional guarantee of sorts was provided to existing parts production in Canada by the provision in the Agreement that Canadian value added in Canadian-assembled vehicles would remain at least at the level achieved during the 1964 model year.[7] As in the United States, independents in Canada could profit from the Agreement provided that they were willing and able to adjust to the opportunities it offered. One possible development, foreseen at the time but apparently not realized to any great extent, was that U.S. vehicle-producers would buy up Canadian independents or set up their own facilities in Canada if the independents' rate of adaption to the new environment was not rapid enough.

3. Employees

Employees in the automotive industries at the time of the Agreement were placed in a position similar to that of the independent parts-producers. Potential gains were possible as a result of greater productivity, but the very rationale for the Agreement meant that these gains would be realized only at the expense of adjustments to an integrated North American automotive industry. For American labour the chief benefit of the Agreement was assurance of a continued growth in the market for exports to Canada, bringing with it the future need for additional workers to supply this market. The rationalization of the industry would involve the transfer of the production of some models and parts to Canada, but any dislocations that arose would probably be minor, and the over-all growth in job opportunities plus the adjustment assistance program would ease the burden.

For Canadian labour the situation was more complex. On the one hand, the adjustments that workers would be called upon to make were considerably greater than for their American counterparts. On the other hand, these workers could anticipate a significant increase in productivity, which the American workers could not, and this would provide ammunition for demands of healthy increases in their wages. Furthermore, the Agreement provided for a more rapid rate of growth in automotive activity in Canada than previously. But here an interesting point arises. By increasing workers' productivity, the Agreement reduced the number of employees required to produce any given level of output. In addition, the amount of capital employed per worker in Canada seems to have been lower than in the United States prior to the Agreement (Chapter 2, Section C). As a result, the Agreement appeared likely to cause a substitu-

---

[7]Paul Wonnacott and R. J. Wonnacott, "The Automotive Agreement of 1965," *Canadian Journal of Economics and Political Science,* May 1967, pp. 273-75. The extent of this transitional protection may have been overstated by the Wonnacotts, since an expansion of assembly operations was possible if inefficiency in parts production was too great.

tion of capital for labour, particularly if labour costs in Canada were to rise towards the U.S. level. Therefore, had it not been for the Can.$260 million fixed growth commitment in the letters of undertaking, employment opportunities in Canadian automotive production might well have fallen relative to what they would have been in the absence of the Agreement.

4. Public Interest

In addition to all the factors outlined above, the Agreement could be expected to provide a solution to a potentially serious strain between Canada and the United States arising from conflicts between the duty-remission plan and U.S. law. There were other economic considerations as well that could affect the general public interest on one side of the border or the other.

There was, on the Canadian side, the fact that automotive duties — estimated at Can.$27 million in 1961 — would have to be foregone.[8] As a result, taxes in Canada might be expected to increase to meet the revenue needs of the government. It will be recalled, however, that the duty-remission plan in Canada (Section B.2, Chapter 3) might have had the same effect.

Offsetting the reduction in customs revenues would be any increase in Canadian automotive producers' profits as a result of a decline in production costs relative to prices. At a minimum, gross profits would increase if the amount of capital employed by the industry in Canada were expanded. As profits expanded, so would the tax revenues of the Canadian government. And since the main Canadian vehicle-manufacturers were subsidiaries of U.S. parents, there might also be an increase in U.S. tax revenues, although this was more complicated to predict because of the way in which foreign earnings of U.S. companies are taxed.

Finally, government expenditures for assisting workers and firms to adjust to the impact of the Agreement would be necessary in the event that transitional dislocations could be proved. The rationale for such assistance is that the burdens of a program designed to be in the general public interest should not have to be borne exclusively by any particular group.

This discussion by no means exhausts all the possible ramifications arising from a marked structural shift in a single sector of the economy, particularly when that sector has as important a role as the motor vehicle industry. Rather than pursue this analysis any further at this point, however, we shall return to it in Chapter 9, after the results of the Agreement to date have been evaluated.

---

[8]Harry G. Johnson, "The New Tariff Policy for the Automotive Industry," University of Western Ontario, *Business Quarterly,* Spring 1964, p. 54.

6

Actual Effects: Integration

A. Integration and Production Shares

In examining the performance of the North American automotive industry during the life of the Agreement, two quite different questions must be raised:

• To what extent has the Agreement contributed to a fuller integration of the Canadian and U.S. sectors of the industry, so that production decisions in either country can be geared to the supply of markets in both?

• How has the Agreement affected the distribution of total North American automotive production between Canada and the United States?

A fundamental point is involved in treating the questions of integration and production shares separately. For reasons that were discussed in detail in Chapters 1 and 2, the Canadian automotive industry, hampered by trade barriers both at home and abroad, was unable to achieve high levels of efficiency in producing a diversified range of products for a small domestic market. A removal of barriers to automotive trade between Canada and the United States would create opportunities for Canada to achieve greater economies of scale and specialization through industrial integration with its natural trading partner — natural, that is, in terms of U.S. ownership of Canadian automotive producers and Canadian consumers' preferences for American-type vehicles. Thus, the elimination of tariffs as a result of the Agreement encouraged fuller integration of North American automotive production and greater efficiency in Canadian operations.

But against the potential efficiency gains to Canada from tariff removal must be placed the potential losses to either country or to both countries arising from the restrictive conditions in the Agreement and the letters of undertaking. These potential losses might arise, in the first instance, because restrictions on free trade in the Agreement limited the extent to which maximum efficiency could be achieved in Canadian automotive production. And if these restrictions, in combination with *market* forces, caused production costs in Canada to continue to be higher than those in the United States, there would be further actual losses from any shift in the existing distribution of total North American automotive production towards Canada arising from the commitments in the letters of undertaking. In the remainder of this chapter we will concentrate upon the efforts of the vehicle-producers to achieve integration, given the constraints that affected their operations; a full discussion of production shares will be the subject of the chapter which follows.

B. Constraints on the Vehicle-Producers

During the four full model years (August 1-July 31) that have passed since President Johnson and Prime Minister Pearson signed the Agreement, the manufacturers faced uncertainties that may have affected their responses somewhat. Basic sourcing decision in this industry must be made annually well in advance of August 1, when production for a new model year traditionally begins. Since the Agreement was not signed until January 16, 1965, such decisions had already been made for the entire 1965 model year and to some extent for the one to follow. Decision-making was also influenced by the fact that legislation implementing the Agreement on the U.S. side was not actually passed by Congress until October, 1965. Even when the Agreement was fully implemented on both sides, some members of Congress remained in opposition to it, and bills to repeal the enabling act in the United States have been introduced annually ever since.[1]

Despite these uncertainties, a fundamental restructuring of North American automotive production since the Agreement is apparent from the statistics that are analyzed in the remainder of this chapter and the next. The manufacturers knew the general outline of the plan well in advance of the January, 1965, signing — their participation in the letters of undertaking was essential — and they appear to have proceeded on the assumption that the Agreement would eventually be applied on the U.S. side and continue to operate in roughly the same form. The

---

[1]The latest was S.2527, *A Bill to Repeal the Automotive Products Act of 1965,* introduced in the Senate on July 1, 1969, by Albert Gore of Tennessee. Similar bills had been brought down in previous years by Senator Gore, who has been a sharp critic of the Agreement from the time it was first brought to the Congress.

remaining limitations on free trade were undoubtedly much more important factors affecting manufacturers' decision-making than uncertainty about continuation of the Agreement.

1. Limitations on Full Integration

Two restrictions in the formal Agreement affected the scope and pace of integration (see Section A.2 of Chapter 4 and Appendix A):

Vehicle Production-to-Sales Ratios in Canada. Integration was permitted within a particular class of vehicles (cars, trucks, buses) but not between classes. Because a manufacturer could not allow the ratio of Canadian vehicle production to vehicle sales in Canada to fall below a fixed percentage (the higher of 75 percent or the ratio in the 1964 model year) for each class, it was impossible to phase out, say, truck assembly in Canada in return for an increase in passenger-car assembly or, for that matter, parts production.

In-Vehicle Canadian Content. The amount of Canadian content in each class of vehicle assembled in Canada could not fall below the level achieved in the 1964 model year. Thus, it was impossible to integrate all parts production immediately, although a rapid rate of growth in Canadian assembly would reduce the significance of this factor.

In combination, these two restrictions tended to favour Canadian assembly over parts production. If the vehicle-production ratios had not existed, integration might have taken a different form; without the in-vehicle content provision, integration could have been more rapid and more complete.

2. Growth Commitments

The letters of undertaking committed vehicle-manufacturers to the following objectives (see Section B of Chapter 4, and Appendix B):

• To expand the amount of Canadian value added by a percentage (60 percent for cars and 50 percent for commercial vehicles) of the increase in the factory cost of vehicles sold in Canada over the level of sales in the 1964 model year.

• To achieve, in addition to the above, an increase of Can.$260 million in Canadian value added by the end of the 1968 model year.[2]

These two conditions placed no limitations on integration but rather guaranteed Canada a particular share in the growth of total North American production. That share could be achieved as efficiently as

---

[2]This amount is the total for all vehicle-manufacturers. Specific commitments for individual companies are shown in Table 9.

possible, given other restrictions in the Agreement, with integration taking any form desired by the vehicle-producer.

The decision facing the vehicle-producers as to how these growth objectives were to be met was influenced by two main factors. First, a decision to expand assembly in Canada beyond what was required to maintain the vehicle production-to-sales ratio would permit the producer to reduce any cost burden arising from the in-vehicle content require- ment (see Section C.2 below). Second, the extent to which assembly in Canada could be expanded was a function of the anticipated growth in the producer's total North American capacity requirements. In order to avoid the costs of idle facilities, increases in Canadian assembly as a result of either greater efficiency through specialization in existing plants or construction of new plants could proceed only as rapidly as these capacity needs. Let us now turn to the reactions of each of the major vehicle-producers to the various constraints they faced.

C. Reactions of the Vehicle-Producers

1. Expansion of Assembly

One of the conclusions that emerges from the post-Agreement record is that while all the vehicle-producers strove to achieve efficiency gains through integration of their North American operations, each of them proceeded along a somewhat different course within the constraints created by the Agreement and the letters of undertaking. Their general approaches are summarized in Table 10, which compares Canadian vehicle production and new vehicle registrations in Canada for each of the major vehicle-producers during calendar years 1960 through 1968.

The importance of Table 10 for our purposes lies in the difference between production and new registrations, with the latter being a proxy for sales.[3]

If the producer chose just to meet the production-to-sales ratio for a particular vehicle class, this difference would not change significantly over time (since it was generally true that there was a balanced position between production and sales during the 1964 model year). This would mean that the producer could reduce the per vehicle Canadian content requirement only to the extent permitted by the growth of sales in Canada. Furthermore, unless per vehicle Canadian content actually increased,

---

[3]Canadian sales statistics are not published for individual producers. Inspection of figures on total sales in Canada of North American-produced vehicles indicates that the new vehicle registrations shown in Table 10 consistently understate, in the aggregate, the level of sales, but the difference is never greater than 5 percent. This difference could be due to a number of factors, including lags in registrations and sales of vehicles for off-highway use which are never registered.

assembly of this class would not contribute to a fulfillment of the fixed growth commitment in the letters of undertaking.[4]

If the producer chose to expand assembly beyond what was required to meet the production-to-sales ratio, the difference would increase over time. In this case the producer could reduce the per vehicle Canadian content requirement more rapidly than he could have on the basis of the growth of sales in Canada. In addition, assembly of this class could also be used to contribute to a fulfillment of the fixed growth commitment in the letters of undertaking.[5]

We will consider the types of integration which have been possible within the general approaches of each producer in turn.

American Motors Corporation provides a special case in the examination of the Agreement's effects on individual producers. American Motors produces cars only, and prior to 1961 it had no reported Canadian vehicle production, indicating that sales in Canada had to be imported over the 17.5 percent tariff. By 1964, the year before the Agreement went into effect, American Motors' production in Canada had reached a level about 10 percent greater than new car registrations there. That same year, 1964, new registrations of American Motors cars reached a peak in Canada, and they declined steadily through 1968.

Despite a flagging sales performance, American Motors expanded Canadian assembly relative to new registrations in Canada to the point where a ratio of nearly two to one was reached during 1968, in an attempt to achieve its fixed growth commitment of Can.$11.2 million. Since American Motors is by far the smallest of the four main car-producers in North America and because of the advantages of large scale in the industry, it may well be that the Agreement continues to prevent possible North American efficiency gains through greater centralization of American Motors' production.[6] But American Motors has sought to make the best of the situation by achieving a notable degree of integration in its North American assembly operations.

The Agreement enabled American Motors to phase out assembly of the Ambassador and Javelin lines completely in Canada, while Canadian assembly of Rebels and Ramblers was expanded. And when the new

---

[4]A decline in per vehicle Canadian content as sales grew in Canada was also possible, consistent with the absolute amount remaining at least as high as during the 1964 model year. In this event the requirements to achieve increased value added in Canada through assembly of another class of vehicle and production or purchase of parts for export would have been even greater.

[5]If per vehicle Canadian content fell too far, assembly would contribute to neither the fixed nor the variable value-added growth requirement in the letters of undertaking.

[6]The Agreement would have permitted American Motors to centralize in Canada, but not in the United States.

TABLE 10

PRODUCTION AND NEW CAR REGISTRATIONS IN CANADA, BY MANUFACTURER, 1960-68

(calendar years)

	1960	1961	1962	1963	1964	1965	1966	1967	1968
American Motors									
Cars: Production	—	8,606	21,928	30,167	35,129	31,347	32,912	33,108	41,726
Registrations	11,132	11,824	20,229	27,019	31,802	31,117	27,448	23,789	21,867
Difference	(11,132)	(3,218)	1,699	3,148	3,327	230	5,464	9,319	19,859
Chrysler									
Cars: Production	50,357	46,726	50,560	86,805	104,734	135,846	172,960	186,675	219,151
Registrations	49,320	47,620	53,443	79,408	100,961	118,232	131,091	139,916	147,020
Difference	1,037	(894)	(2,883)	7,397	3,773	17,614	41,869	46,759	72,131
Trucks: Production	5,988	6,496	6,390	9,691	13,062	17,340	16,691	16,137	16,573
Registrations	5,413	6,079	6,149	8,376	11,147	14,640	16,133	15,303	15,819
Difference	575	417	241	1,315	1,915	2,700	558	834	754
Ford									
Cars: Production	94,166	97,907	118,190	142,273	153,243	169,176	198,498	177,316	287,286
Registrations	85,075	97,000	115,058	126,450	150,945	161,879	165,678	156,202	183,127
Difference	9,091	907	3,132	15,823	2,298	7,297	32,820	21,114	104,159
Trucks: Production	19,167	16,967	25,562	33,341	37,136	43,756	97,149	118,463	157,815
Registrations	14,671	16,711	21,078	25,634	29,708	31,309	38,746	43,371	49,878
Difference	4,496	256	4,484	7,707	7,428	12,447	58,403	75,092	107,937

TABLE 10 (continued)

General Motors

Cars:	Production	175,086	167,375	229,639	264,341	246,466	351,303	285,984	311,514	338,016
	Registrations	169,617	173,015	225,454	246,200	246,113	289,694	280,077	264,681	269,782
	Difference	5,469	(5,640)	4,185	18,141	353	61,609	5,907	46,833	68,234
Trucks:	Production	34,319	28,850	37,579	43,883	47,123	68,420	69,647	73,405	86,288
	Registrations	31,081	30,669	35,041	40,073	45,694	50,390	54,200	52,668	55,274
	Difference	3,238	(1,819)	2,538	3,810	1,429	18,030	15,447	20,737	31,014

International Harvester

Trucks:	Production	10,566	10,590	10,285	11,539	11,795	13,189	12,772	14,175	13,215
	Registrations	11,978	11,464	11,074	10,738	11,318	12,572	12,721	12,589	10,063
	Difference	(1,412)	(874)	(789)	801	477	617	51	1,586	3,152

Sources: Production: *Facts and Figures of the Automotive Industry* (Toronto: Motor Vehicle Manufacturers' Association (Canada), various issues).

Registrations: R. L. Polk & Co. (Canada) Ltd., as quoted in *ibid.*

American Motors compact car, the Hornet, was brought out in 1969 — at which time the Rambler line was discontinued — an interesting example of regional specialization in assembly was introduced. All sales of Hornets in eastern Canada and the eastern United States are supplied from American Motors' plant in Brampton, Ontario; sales in western regions are supplied from the plant in Kenosha, Wisconsin.[7]

Chrysler Corporation has clearly chosen to concentrate on increased car assemblies as a means of meeting the Can.$33 million fixed growth commitment in its letter of undertaking.[8] Indeed, Table 10 suggests that if Chrysler met the production-to-sales ratio for trucks, it did so with little margin to spare in the years 1966 through 1968. Canadian car production by Chrysler, on the other hand, had risen to a level equal to one-and-a-half times new registrations in Canada during 1968.

By 1968, Chrysler had integrated its North American assembly operations by phasing out all Canadian assembly of the Chrysler and Valiant lines, concentrating on Canadian production of Polara and Monaco models in the Dodge line and on Plymouth Fury models. During 1969 Chrysler began assembling Darts in substantial quantity in Canada, and the company has indicated that in the future there will be a greater concentration in Canada on Darts and Valiants, the latter being reinstated after having been phased out in Canada initially.

Ford Motor Company was faced with a Can.$74.2 million fixed growth commitment in its letter of undertaking with the Canadian government. Prior to 1968, Ford sought to contribute to this commitment by accelerating very rapidly the production of trucks in Canada. This trend developed to such a point, in fact, that less than one of every three trucks produced in 1968 was required to meet new registrations in Canada during that year.

In 1968 Ford also became a large net exporter of cars. Even before 1968 there had been an integration of car operations, with production of Comets and Fairlanes being completely phased out in Canada as of 1967. In 1968 and 1969, Ford began a program to achieve even greater integration of its car operations in North America. First, soon after its new St. Thomas, Ontario, plant went into operation in late 1967, Falcon production was shifted there from the Oakville, Ontario, plant. Then, in March, 1969, the operations in the St. Thomas plant were shifted from Falcon to Maverick production. As in the case with American Motors' new compact Hornet, Ford achieves a degree of regional specialization in the North American production of the Maverick, with an

---

[7]Edward Cowan, "Auto-Trade Pact Gets Tune-Up," *New York Times,* November 12, 1969, p. 59.
[8]Chrysler's letter is reproduced as Appendix B in Part IV of this study.

estimated 70 percent of total requirements being supplied from Canada and the remainder being supplied from Ford's Kansas City plant. Finally, beginning with production for the 1970 model year, Fairlane assembly was reinstated at Ford's Oakville plant to meet increased North American capacity requirements for this model.

General Motors Corporation appears to have relied much more heavily upon increased parts exports to meet its commitments than have any of the other producers. Production of cars and trucks has expanded faster than new registrations in Canada, but the increase has been much smaller than for Chrysler and Ford, both absolutely and, even more significantly, relative to the size of General Motors' Canadian operations. Integration of car production is suggested, however, by the fact that there has been a relative decline in Buick, Pontiac, and Oldsmobile operations in Canada, coupled with an expansion of Chevrolet assembly. In total, General Motors has reduced the number of car models produced in Canada to about one-half the pre-Agreement level.

General Motors was committed to Can.$121 million of the total Can.$260 million minimum increase in Canadian value added that was agreed to in the letters of undertaking. The comparatively small increase in General Motors' car and truck assembly in Canada can be taken as an indication that expanded parts exports must have been a major factor in the achievement of this commitment. It may also suggest that General Motors' assembly operations in Canada compared more favourably in terms of the level of costs in the United States prior to the Agreement than did the assembly activities of the other Canadian producers, a factor, no doubt, of the scale of General Motors' Canadian activities.

International Harvester's Canadian truck operations declined relative to new registrations in Canada during 1965 and 1966. There may have been some difficulty for this company in achieving the production-to-sales requirement in 1965, but we cannot be certain. Since production has not increased very significantly since 1964, the ability of this company to realize efficiency gains by reducing Canadian content per vehicle has undoubtedly been quite limited, owing to the need to maintain the 1964 level of content in Canadian-produced trucks. Furthermore, International Harvester probably had to rely upon parts exports to achieve its commitments in the letter of undertaking, but we have been unable to determine the specific commitment for this firm.

Summarizing to this point, the vehicle-producers were generally able to achieve a significant degree of integration in their North American assembly operations within the constraints they faced. Entire lines were phased out in Canada, permitting greater realization of economies of specialization. The choice as to what vehicles would be assembled in

Canada was based primarily upon North American capacity requirements for particular models. The pattern of growth in total Canadian assembly, on the other hand, varied considerably among the firms, and the factors affecting this growth were a combination of comparative costs, capacity needs, and constraints in the Agreement and the letters of undertaking.

2. Effects of the In-Vehicle Content Requirement

In Section B.1 of this chapter we discussed why the in-vehicle Canadian content requirement contained in the Agreement was a constraint on effective integration of North American operations. The vehicle production-to-sales ratios and the letters of undertaking may have prevented the realization of maximum efficiency in North America, but they did not in themselves hamper efficiency in Canada, whereas the in-vehicle content requirement did. One interpretation of the producers' efforts to expand Canadian vehicle assembly would be that, by so doing, they tended to minimize the cost burden of this provision. The purpose of this section is to examine further the implications of the in-vehicle content provision.

Let us suppose that the manufacturers had relied exclusively upon growth in Canadian vehicle demand, as measured by new registrations, to reduce the level of per vehicle content in Canadian production. We will also assume, for simplicity, that the producers achieved exactly 60 percent Canadian content in cars and 50 percent in trucks sold in Canada during the 1964 calendar year. On the basis of these assumptions, Table 11 enables us to compute an estimate of what required per vehicle Canadian content would have been in the 1968 calendar year.

Part A of Table 11 shows the ratio of new registrations in 1968 divided by those in 1964 for each of the producers listed in Table 10. Assuming that assembly in Canada had grown by no more than this amount, Part B shows the estimated per vehicle Canadian content that would have been required in 1968. The results in Part B are derived by dividing the figures in Part A into 0.6 in the case of cars and 0.5 in the case of trucks.[9] American Motors and International Harvester require a special word because registrations were lower in 1968 than in 1964 for both. Evidently there was to be a downward adjustment in the total in-vehicle content requirement in the event of a sales decline, so we assume that the same estimated per vehicle content requirement applied

---

[9]We are assuming here that the per unit value of vehicles has not changed over the period. Any increase in value lowers the figures in Part B; a decrease raises them. With per unit values held constant, *total* in-vehicle content required was 0.6 times a constant for cars and 0.5 times a constant for trucks in both 1964 and 1968.

in 1968 as in 1964 — 60 percent for American Motors cars and 50 percent for International Harvester trucks.[10]

Table 11 indicates that just by expanding Canadian assembly at the same pace as new registrations, Canadian content per vehicle could have been reduced sharply for Chrysler car and Ford truck production. Reductions in other instances were quite limited on the basis of demand growth in Canada alone.

TABLE 11

ESTIMATES OF REQUIRED PER VEHICLE CANADIAN CONTENT
BASED ON SALES GROWTH IN CANADA

Part A: New Registrations in 1968 Divided by New Registrations in 1964.

	Cars	Trucks
American Motors	0.69	—
Chrysler	1.46	1.42
Ford	1.21	2.02
General Motors	1.10	1.38
International Harvester	—	0.89

Part B: Estimated Canadian Content Required per Vehicle in 1968 as a Result of Demand Growth (percentages).

	Cars	Trucks
American Motors	60	—
Chrysler	41	35
Ford	50	25
General Motors	55	36
International Harvester	—	50

Sources: Part A: Computed from Table 10.
Part B: Results in Part A divided into 0.6 for cars and 0.5 for trucks except for American Motors and International Harvester. For these companies it is assumed that owing to a sales decline the total amount of in-vehicle content required was reduced to maintain a constant per vehicle commitment. See footnote 9 and text for details.

It is interesting, although probably coincidental, that the path that each of the three main producers appears to have chosen in meeting the commitments in the letters of undertaking was consistent with the one suggested by Canadian demand conditions (see Section C.1 above). Ford concentrated, at least initially, on trucks; Chrysler on cars; and General Motors apparently more on parts. The results of increased assembly in Canada beyond what was needed to match demand growth are shown in Table 12.

---

[10]The only reference we have been able to find concerning this provision is contained in General Motors' letter of undertaking, but we assume that it applied to all producers. See *Hearings on H.R. 9042 . . ., op. cit.,* p. 46. If American Motors or International Harvester experienced an increase in the *value* of sales even though *unit* sales in Canada declined, there would still have been an opportunity to reduce the per vehicle content required, but we have been unable to obtain statistics that are relevant to this question.

Part A in Table 12 corresponds to Part A in Table 11 and shows the level of production in 1968 divided by that in 1964 for each of the main vehicle-producers. If we again assume that the producers achieved exactly 60 percent Canadian content in cars and 50 percent in trucks produced in Canada during the 1964 calendar year, Part B of Table 12 shows the estimated per vehicle Canadian content required in 1968.[11] Once again, American Motors and International Harvester require special treatment. Because these firms experienced a sales decline during this period, we have reduced the total in-vehicle content requirement accordingly.[12]

As a result of the growth in vehicle assembly that has occurred since the Agreement, it would appear from Table 12 that Ford's car and truck operations in Canada are no longer seriously hampered by the Agreement's minimum content requirement.[13] The same may be said for Chrysler's car production. The high per vehicle content still

TABLE 12

ESTIMATES OF REQUIRED PER VEHICLE CANADIAN CONTENT
BASED ON PRODUCTION GROWTH IN CANADA

Part A: Production in 1968 Divided by Production in 1964.

	Cars	Trucks
American Motors	1.19	—
Chrysler	2.09	1.27
Ford	1.88	4.25
General Motors	1.37	1.83
International Harvester	—	1.12

Part B: Estimated Canadian Content Required per Vehicle in 1968 as a Result of Production Growth (percentages).

	Cars	Trucks
American Motors	35	—
Chrysler	28	39
Ford	32	12
General Motors	44	27
International Harvester	—	40

Sources: Part A: Computed from Table 10.
Part B: Result in Part A divided into 0.6 for cars and 0.5 for trucks except for American Motors and International Harvester, for whom adjustments were made to reflect reductions in total in-vehicle content required owing to sales declines. See footnotes 9 and 12, and text for details.

---

[11]The points raised in footnote 9 apply here as well. We have treated production and registrations as being equal in 1964, which we see from Table 10 to be invalid. The bias this introduces is quite small in most cases, however, and does not affect the conclusions that are reached in the text.

[12]For example, American Motors' registrations in 1968 were 69 percent of the 1964 level (see Table 11, Part A). Multiplying 0.6 times .69, we obtain .414. Dividing 1.19 (Table 12, Part A) into .414 yields the estimate of 35 percent shown in Part B of Table 12. A similar calculation was applied to International Harvester.

required in Chrysler's truck production suggests that if this content level represented a major cost burden prior to the Agreement, it is still likely to do so.[14]

General Motors has reduced per vehicle content requirements in its truck production to about half the pre-Agreement level. The fact that General Motors' car operations continue to require a considerable amount of Canadian content per vehicle may represent a continuing cost burden. But this company had advantages of large size in Canada to begin with, and the specialization in parts production that accompanied specialization in car assembly may have been sufficient to reduce any excess costs in required Canadian content without as great a reduction in the per vehicle content as was achieved by the other firms.

The truck production of International Harvester still requires a high per vehicle content, and this probably constitutes a continuing cost disadvantage for this company. In the case of American Motors, in-vehicle content required was reduced significantly, but this was due primarily to the fact that the total requirement fell as a result of a decline in Canadian sales during the period.

D. Integration and Trade

1. Growth in Total Automotive Trade

We have been concentrating our attention to this point on the efforts of individual producers to integrate North American automotive production subject to the constraints in the Agreement and the letters of undertaking. The level of bilateral trade provides one of the best indicators of the combined results of these efforts.

It will be recalled from Chapter 1 that prior to Canada's pilot duty-remission plan (October, 1962) there was little integration in North

---

[13]Ford, it turns out, received a special concession in its negotiations with the Canadian government. In response to the duty-remission plan in Canada, Ford had planned to integrate its North American engine production by reducing the number of engine types produced in its Windsor plant. Most of the expanded production in Windsor would be exported, with an accompanying increase in engine imports of other types. Canada granted a reduction in the minimum Canadian content requirement to account for this, but failed to communicate this fact to its own Auditor-General. The latter, making a strict interpretation of the Agreement, claimed Ford owed Can.$75 million in duties for failing to meet its commitments. It seems fairly certain from our analysis that by 1968 Ford no longer required this special concession. See *Hearings on H.R. 9042 ...*, *op. cit.*, pp. 51-52, for Ford's letter to the Canadian government explaining its position.

[14]Recall that the particular requirement we have been discussing would allow for specialization *within* parts production as the number of models was reduced. But as long as the requirement translates into high per vehicle content, there is little room to specialize *between* parts — say by making all clutches in Canada and all transmissions in the United States — and this was a primary factor in making Canadian operations more efficient.

American automotive production, since trade flowed essentially one way. U.S. exports were concentrated in parts that could be entered into Canada duty-free if content requirements (Table 3) were met, although some low-volume, high-price vehicles were shipped to Canada over the tariff. Canada, meanwhile, was unable to find a regular market in the United States, since its automotive industry was hampered by high costs owing to a failure to achieve economies of scale and specialization — a result, in part, of the U.S. tariff barrier. Table 13, showing Canada's automotive trade with the United States for calendar years 1960 through 1968, demonstrates how much that picture has changed in the past few years.[15]

Table 13 shows that Canadian imports and exports did increase during the years in which the duty-remission plans were in operation (1963 and 1964), but this increase was insignificant compared with that since the Agreement went into effect in 1965. The figures do suggest, however, that these plans may have provided the platform which allowed the Agreement to get off to such a rapid start. Immediately in 1965, both Canadian exports and imports increased sharply. The increase gained momentum, and by 1968, the fourth year of the Agreement, exports had expanded more than tenfold, and imports more than fourfold, over 1964.

2. Trade by Product Class

a) *Completed Vehicles*

Table 14 indicates the rapid increase in the integration of North American vehicle production following the Agreement.[16] Part A of this table shows that the degree to which U.S.-produced vehicles have penetrated the Canadian market has increased from 2.4 percent in 1964 to 41.1 percent in 1968.

Import penetration has been somewhat greater for cars, reaching 43.4 percent in 1968. For convertibles alone the figure reached 69.5 percent that year. In the case of trucks, import penetration reached 31.1 percent in 1968. An interesting point which emerges from the complete tables in Appendix D of Part IV is that import penetration has been much more pronounced for light-weight than for medium-weight trucks, and then reaches the highest levels for the heavier-truck categories.

---

[15]Table 13 is based on Canadian import and export statistics. For reasons to be discussed in Chapter 7, these statistics are not adequate for an analysis of changes in the *balance* of trade between the two countries. They are suited for demonstrating the orders of magnitude involved in the *growth* of trade and therefore the degree of integration, which is our purpose here.
[16]Appendix D in Part IV of this study provides tables showing how trade has developed for various automotive body styles (e.g., station wagons, hardtops, etc.). The purpose of these tables is to show variations in the degree of import penetration and production in Canada for export markets. It should be stressed, however, that vehicle-producers integrated their operations in terms of product lines (e.g., Mavericks, Darts, etc., in Canada), and the impact on body styles was mostly secondary.

TABLE 13

CANADA'S AUTOMOTIVE TRADE WITH THE UNITED STATES, 1960-68
(values in thousand dollars Canadian)

	Total Automotive Exports		Total Automotive Imports	
Calendar Year	Units	Value	Units	Value
1960	187	4,248	33,684	407,155
1961	193	9,190	24,114	398,012
1962	1,136	15,541	23,500	519,251
1963	3,504	40,168	11,800	604,077
1964	19,094	99,380	18,469	716,675
1965	51,146	233,097	53,655	1,012,210
1966	243,206	844,996	131,582	1,501,303
1967	496,904	1,586,706	276,756	2,109,288
1968	731,455	2,434,981	365,636	2,881,357

	Car Exports		Car Imports	
	Units	Value	Units	Value
1960	179	424	27,841	63,540
1961	175	400	16,574	47,953
1962	150	322	17,878	54,314
1963	319	639	7,372	28,636
1964	10,950	20,822	15,138	44,294
1965	31,692	66,216	46,108	125,432
1966	146,794	346,378	114,748	315,479
1967	310,974	816,002	238,628	662,641
1968	472,508	1,257,042	308,359	896,700

	Commercial-Vehicle Exports		Commercial-Vehicle Imports	
	Units	Value	Units	Value
1960	8	39	5,843	26,745
1961	18	40	7,540	23,329
1962	986	2,494	5,622	23,860
1963	3,185	3,171	4,428	20,737
1964	8,144	5,122	3,331	22,900
1965	19,454	23,886	7,547	45,029
1966	96,412	146,196	16,834	93,086
1967	185,930	289,276	38,128	144,538
1968	258,947	428,656	57,277	195,809

	Parts Exports	Parts Imports
	Value	Value
1960	3,785	316,870
1961	8,749	326,730
1962	11,038	441,077
1963	36,358	554,704
1964	73,436	649,481
1965	142,995	841,749
1966	352,422	1,092,738
1967	481,428	1,302,109
1968	749,283	1,788,848

Sources: Dominion Bureau of Statistics, Cat. Nos. 65-004 and 65-007, as quoted in
Facts and Figures of the Automotive Industry (Toronto: Motor Vehicle
Manufacturers' Association (Canada), various issues).

TABLE 14

Trade in Completed Vehicles, 1960-68
(calendar years)

	1960	1961	1962	1963	1964	1965	1966	1967	1968

Part A: Market Shares in Canada of Factory Shipments of Vehicles Imported to Canada from the United States[a,b] (percentages)

	1960	1961	1962	1963	1964	1965	1966	1967	1968
Total all vehicles	7.0	5.1	3.6	1.2	2.4	6.3	17.8	37.5	41.1
Cars	7.9	4.8	4.0	1.4	2.7	6.7	19.2	40.5	43.4
Trucks	2.7	6.5	1.2	0.4	0.4	4.0	11.2	24.2	30.4

Part B: Unit Shipments for Export as a Percentage of Total Unit Factory Shipments of Made-in-Canada Vehicles (percentages)

	1960	1961	1962	1963	1964	1965	1966	1967	1968
Total all vehicles	5.8	3.3	3.5	3.3	6.7	11.3	31.5	51.3	59.4
Cars	5.7	2.9	3.3	3.0	6.7	10.4	28.3	49.8	58.0
Trucks	6.3	5.6	4.9	4.6	6.7	16.3	42.1	56.8	64.3

Part C: Ratio of Unit Export Shipments of Made-in-Canada Vehicles to Unit Factory Shipments of Vehicles Imported to Canada from the United States[b]

	1960	1961	1962	1963	1964	1965	1966	1967	1968
Total all vehicles	.82	.63	.98	2.64	2.97	1.89	2.12	1.75	2.10
Cars	.72	.59	.80	2.19	2.55	1.60	1.67	1.46	1.80
Trucks	2.45	.85	4.30	11.51	19.85	4.71	5.76	4.11	4.12

[a]Total market equals shipments of imports from the United States plus domestic shipments of made-in-Canada vehicles.

[b]Imports exclude direct imports by final purchaser (for which full duties have to be paid).

Source: Computed from Dominion Bureau of Statistics, Cat. No. 42-002, as quoted in *Facts and Figures of the Automotive Industry* (Toronto: Motor Vehicle Manufacturers' Association (Canada), various issues).

The Agreement places one condition on a producer's Canadian assembly operations: the ratio, in terms of net sales value, of vehicles produced in Canada to vehicles sold in Canada must be at least as high as during the 1964 model year. Therefore, each advance in the degree of import penetration has to be matched by at least an equal increase in Canadian production for export markets. Part B of Table 14 shows the distribution of Canadian vehicle production between domestic and export shipments.[17]

In 1968, Canadian manufacturers exported six of every ten vehicles they produced, compared with only one of every fifteen in 1964, the year prior to the Agreement. The increase has been a little greater for trucks than for cars, chiefly because of the sharp increase in Ford's truck assembly in Canada (Table 10).

Part C of Table 14 combines the results of Parts A and B by computing the ratio of shipments of Canadian-produced vehicles for export to shipments of vehicles imported from the United States. An entry which is greater than one indicates Canadian exports exceed shipments of imports; an entry which is less than one indicates the reverse. The fact that exports have exceeded imports by a wide margin since the Agreement — and actually since the first duty-remission plan was introduced in Canada in October, 1962 — reflects in part the efforts of the producers to meet the constraints that Canada continues to place on duty-free trade, which were examined in Section C.1 of this chapter.

b) *Parts*

Table 13 showed that exports of automotive parts and accessories from Canada to the United States were more than ten times greater in 1968 than in 1964. Canadian imports of these products from the United States started from a much higher base, but the 1968 level was still over three times the 1964 level. Detailed analysis of shifts in production that have accompanied this expansion of trade is complicated by the very large number of automotive parts and by the difficulty of obtaining comparable statistics in the two countries. Therefore, in this brief section we will confine our analysis to parts and accessories imported duty-free into the United States from Canada under the provisions of the Agreement.

Table 15 lists the categories of the U.S. imports valued in excess of $1 million in 1968. Values for the period January 18 to December 31, 1965, are also shown for comparison.[18] Vehicle-manufacturers were not restricted in terms of how they might meet the commitments in the letters of undertaking. This table, then, indicates those items which could be produced at the lowest cost in Canada for the entire North American market. It does not necessarily indicate, however, whether Canada could produce these items at a lower cost than in the United States, since some expansion of parts exports may have been required to meet the commitments to expand Canadian value added.

[17]Since this condition could be met by exporting anywhere, Part B of Table 14 shows total Canadian exports rather than those to the United States alone.
[18]Comparable figures prior to the effective date of tariff modifications in the United States are not available.

E. Summary

The Automotive Agreement has produced a marked increase in the integration of the North American automotive industry. Trade flows have been expanded many times over, both at an aggregate level and for separate automotive-product classes. Two sets of statistics indicate dramatically the extent to which production decisions in both countries have already become geared to total North American needs:

• Imports from the United States accounted for more than 40 percent of the Canadian market for North American-produced vehicles in 1968, compared with under 3 percent in 1964.

• About 60 percent of all vehicles produced in Canada during 1968 were exported, compared with less than 7 percent in 1964.

Possibilities for efficiency gains have accompanied this increased integration, as evidenced by

1) reductions in the number of vehicle lines produced in Canada;

2) substantially higher volumes for the lines that Canadian producers have selected for specialization; and

3) possibilities for lower Canadian content per vehicle assembled in Canada, leading to some reduction in the low-volume parts production needed to meet the former (pre-Agreement) content requirements.

In the next chapter we shall analyze the available evidence to determine the extent to which this expansion of integration has been accompanied by changes in the shares of automotive activity being conducted in Canada and the United States.

TABLE 15

U.S. Imports of Parts from Canada Admitted
Duty-Free under the Automotive Agreement and Having
a Value of at Least $1,000,000 in Calendar 1968

TSUSA[a] Number	Brief Description	Imports Jan. 18[b] to Dec. 31, 1965 ($'000)	Calendar 1968 ($'000)
613.1900	Pipe and tube fittings of copper alloy	0	1,169.6
646.7900	Staples, rivets, bolts, and other fasteners	227.8	4,376.2
647.0200	Hinges, fittings, and mountings	1,488.6	14,739.8
652.8500	Springs and leaves for springs of base metal	11,298.4	34,947.3
652.8900	Other springs	0	1,292.2
660.4500	Piston-type engines	15,767.8	184,764.0
660.5100	Cast-iron parts for internal-combustion engines	6,675.6	8,276.4
660.5300	Parts of piston-type engines other than combustion-ignition engines	18,933.1	26,976.5
660.9500	Pumps for liquids	1,895.7	4,506.9
661.1100	Fans and blowers	82.7	2,206.4
661.2100	Air-conditioning machines	297.1	1,132.7
678.5100	Machines, miscellaneous	0	1,285.6
680.2800	Taps, cocks, valves	76.7	1,501.0
680.3400	Ball bearings with integral shafts	177.7	1,294.7
680.3600	Other ball and roller bearings	262.4	1,478.1
682.6500	Generators, motors, electric under 200 horsepower	31.2	1,383.5
683.1100	Lead-acid-type storage batteries	52.0	1,612.9
683.6100	Electrical starting and ignition equipment	696.5	9,614.3
683.6600	Electrical lighting equipment	518.3	5,808.3
685.5520	Radio receivers	} 2,236.0[c]	{ 17,780.6
685.5540	Other radiotelegraphic apparatus		{ 4,657.9
685.9100	Electrical switches, relays, etc.	63.0	1,087.7
686.1100	Resistors	0	1,236.7
688.1300	Ignition wiring sets	2,248.0	11,795.3
688.1600	Insulated electrical conductors	n.a.	2,424.8
692.2500	Cast-iron parts	480.5	2,323.4
692.2810	Body stampings	}	9,369.9
692.2820	Bumpers		24,821.3
692.2830	Wheels for mounting		16,461.7
692.2840	Hubcaps and wheel covers	} 38,763.7[d]	9,890.9
692.2850	Radiators		17,689.3
692.2860	Mufflers and tailpipes		2,122.3
692.2870	Other parts, including truck tractors	}	231,069.9
727.0700	Furniture for vehicles	6,215,9	44,633.3
772.6600	Hose, pipe, and tubing	184.6	1,610.6
772.8600	Closures, including caps and lids	0	1,063.7
773.2600	Gaskets	151.7	3,299.1
774.700	Miscellaneous rubber products	0	1,041.7

n.a. Not available.
[a]TSUSA — Tariff Schedule of the United States.
[b]January 18, 1965, was the effective date for tariff modifications under the Agreement.
[c]The equivalent figure for 1968 was $22,438.5.
[d]The equivalent figure for 1968 was $311,420.3.

Sources: *Third Annual Report of the President to the Congress on the Operation of the Automotive Products Trade Act of 1965* (Washington: Government Printing Office, 1969), pp. 19-20. Also *Second Annual Report . . ., op. cit.,* pp. 45-50.

7

Actual Effects: Production Shares

One of the primary objectives the Canadian government had in mind when it negotiated the Agreement was to narrow the gap between the value of Canadian automotive production and the value of Canadian purchases of North American-produced motor vehicles.[1] The goal to close this gap is not spelled out explicitly in the formal Agreement between the two countries.[2] In fact, that document by itself would permit just the opposite result. In return for protection of its assembly operations, Canada commits manufacturers to no more than the same total value added in Canada as they achieved in the 1964 model year, as well as to the 1964 model-year ratio between Canadian assembly and total automotive sales there. On this basis, the gap could have been widened in both absolute

---

[1]This gap has usually been expressed as one between Canada's shares of North American automotive production and sales, respectively 4.5 percent and 7.5 percent prior to the Agreement. These figures have been repeated so often in Canada that they have come to be accepted as fact, although the basis for them is unknown. In Table 4, Chapter 3, we see that reported value added in the automotive industries of North America was U.S.$13,409 million in 1963, with Canada accounting for U.S.$709 million, or 5.3 percent. That same year Canada had net purchases of about U.S.$522 million in automotive products from the United States (computed from Table 13, Chapter 6). Adding these net purchases to the value added in Canada yields U.S.$1,231 million, or 9.1 percent of total North American production. In other words, we would conclude that Canada's share of North American automotive production and sales was roughly 5.3 percent and 9.1 percent, respectively, in 1963.

[2]One of the objectives stated in the Agreement (see Article I (b) in Appendix A) was to enable "the industries of both countries to participate on a fair and equitable basis in the expanding market of the two countries." The Canadian government apparently interprets "fair and equitable" to mean a situation in which the production-sales gap disappears. If a criterion of strict balance between purchases and production were to be applied generally, of course, the traditional incentive for trade, comparative advantages in the production of different products, would not operate. We will explore this point in more detail in Chapters 9 and 10.

and relative terms as automotive sales in Canada increased, because total value added there was not obliged to grow.

This prospect was altered fundamentally, however, by the letters of undertaking between the vehicle-manufacturers and the Canadian government. These ensured that the value of automotive production in Canada would grow at roughly the same rate, relative to sales, as in the past, *plus* an additional Can.$260 million (U.S.$241 million) by the end of the 1968 model year (see Table 9). It was this fixed commitment, independent of sales growth, which contributed to the Canadian objective — fundamental, though unstated in the formal Agreement — of narrowing the production-sales gap from what it would have been under the old tariff structure.[3]

With this background we turn now to an analysis of changes in the distribution of automotive production activity in North America following the Agreement. Our main objective will be to determine whether or not the production-sales gap in Canada has responded as one would have expected on the basis of the various commitments in the Agreement and — more to the point — those in the letters of undertaking.

A. Distribution of Vehicle Production

Table 16 presents motor-vehicle-production figures for the United States and Canada during the years 1960 to 1968. The last column in this table computes Canada's share of North American output of cars, trucks and buses, and total vehicles. (We will disregard the "required" heading for the moment.) Except in the truck and bus category in 1961, Canada's share has increased continuously throughout this period. By 1968 Canada's share of total vehicle production was a little more than double the 1960 level; the share of truck and bus production has grown by somewhat more than Canada's share of car production.

The growth in Canada's share of vehicle production prior to 1965 reflects a faster rate of growth of sales in Canada and, after 1962, the impact of Canada's duty-remission plans, although we cannot separate the effects of these two factors. After 1965, however, the growth in Canada's share was due primarily to the response of manufacturers seeking to meet their commitments in the letters of undertaking. This conclusion is based on a comparison of the "actual" and "required" headings in Table 16.

The Agreement contains the proviso that to qualify for duty-free treatment, a Canadian manufacturer must maintain a production-to-sales

---

[3]We have seen in Chapter 3 that Canada's full duty-remission plan, introduced in October, 1963, might also have reduced the gap, but this was problematical. The letters of undertaking removed the uncertainty.

TABLE 16

NORTH AMERICAN VEHICLE PRODUCTION, 1960-68

(thousand units)

Calendar Year	United States	Canada Actual	Canada Required[a]	Total	Canada's Share of Total (%) Actual	Canada's Share of Total (%) Required[a]
Cars						
1960	6,703.1	325.8		7,028.9	4.63	
1961	5,522.0	323.6		5.845.6	5.53	
1962	6,943.3	424.6		7,367.9	5.76	
1963	7,644.4	532.2		8,176.6	6.51	
1964	7,745.5	559.6		8,305.1	6.74	
1965	9,335.2	706.8	(685.0)	10,042.0	7.04	(6.82)
1966	8,604.7	701.5	(677.8)	9,306.2	7.54	(7.28)
1967	7,412.7	720.8	(654.1)	8,133.5	8.86	(8.04)
1968	8,848.6	900.9	(689.0)	9,749.3	9.24	(7.07)
Trucks and Buses						
1960	1,202.0	72.0		1,274.0	5.65	
1961	1,130.9	63.3		1,194.2	5.30	
1962	1,254.0	80.6		1,334.6	6.04	
1963	1,464.4	99.1		1,563.5	6.34	
1964	1,562.4	111.4		1,673.8	7.13	
1965	1,802.6	139.8	(124.5)	1,942.4	7.20	(6.41)
1966	1,791.6	200.6	(135.3)	1,992.2	10.07	(6.79)
1967	1,611.1	226.4	(138.1)	1,837.5	12.32	(7.52)
1968	1,971.7	279.1	(147.4)	2,250.8	12.40	(6.55)
Total						
1960	7,905.1	397.8		8,302.9	4.79	
1961	6,652.9	386.9		7,039.8	5.50	
1962	8,197.3	505.2		8,702.5	5.81	
1963	9,108.8	631.4		9,740.2	6.48	
1964	9,307.9	671.0		9,978.9	6.72	(6.75)
1965	11,137.8	846.6	(809.5)	11,984.4	7.06	(7.20)
1966	10,396.3	902.1	(813.1)	11,298.4	7.98	(7.20)
1967	9,023.8	947.2	(792.2)	9,971.0	9.50	(7.95)
1968	10,820.3	1,180.0	(836.4)	11,996.1	9.84	(6.97)

[a]For an explanation of how these results were derived, see text.

Source: *Facts and Figures of the Automotive Industry* (Toronto: Motor Vehicle Manufacturers' Association (Canada) various issues).

ratio for vehicles in Canada at least as high as that attained during the 1964 model year. This ratio was, in the aggregate, 1.081 for cars and 1.036 for trucks and buses.[4] Assuming that growth in numbers parallels growth in sales value, for the latter is the basis for determining fulfillment, we multiply these ratios by unit sales in Canada to obtain the production

---

[4]In the 1964 model year, 593,233 cars and 109,742 trucks and buses were produced in Canada, while 548,737 cars and 105,939 trucks and buses of Canadian or U.S. origin were sold there. This information was supplied by the Dominion Bureau of Statistics through Canada's Department of Industry.

in Canada needed to just meet the production-to-sales condition.[5] The results are shown in brackets in Table 16. The difference between what was required and what actually took place reflects the use of vehicle-assembling to fulfill other requirements of the Agreement or the letters of undertaking (see Section C.1, Chapter 6). As Table 16 shows, had it not been for increased assembly beyond what was required under the first condition of the formal agreement, Canada's share of North American vehicle production would have been nearly the same in 1968 as in 1964.[6]

Charts 2 and 3 depict the production figures presented in Table 16. The vertical scale in these charts is ten times greater for Canada than for the United States, roughly correcting for the different sizes of the two countries in terms of population and vehicle sales. In other words, when the two lines showing production in the two countries intersect, Canadian output is equal to one-tenth the level of U.S. output.[7]

From Chart 2 we see that the differential between Canadian and U.S. car production has narrowed steadily since 1960. In 1968 Canada was producing, for the first time, more than 10 percent as many cars as the United States. The same trend is seen for trucks and buses (Chart 2) and all vehicles (Chart 3), but the intersection point occurred in 1965 in the case of the former and in 1967 for the latter.

B. Distribution of Automotive Employment

It would be possible for the increase in Canada's share of North American vehicle production to be accompanied by a declining share of parts and accessories production. Comparable statistics on parts and accessories output do not exist for the two countries, so in this section we

---

[5]Sales in Canada of Canadian and U.S. vehicles were as follows:

Calendar Year	Cars	Trucks and Buses	Total
1965	633,641	120,205	753,846
1966	626,986	130,629	757,615
1967	605,049	133,330	738,379
1968	637,393	142,241	779,634

Source: Dominion Bureau of Statistics, Cat. No. 63-007, as quoted in *Facts and Figures of the Automotive Industry* (Toronto: Motor Vehicle Manufacturers' Association (Canada), various issues). The ratio we are using here would be subject to change as market shares of individual firms varied, but we are unable to correct for this factor. The bias this introduces to the analysis is not significant.

[6]This is conjecture, of course, since we do not know what would have happened if the duty-remission plan or some other alternative had been in effect during this period.

[7]Note that in terms of Canada's share of total North American production, shown in Table 16, intersection points in these charts indicate that Canada's share is one-eleventh or about 9.1 percent of the total.

Chart 2

NORTH AMERICAN CAR AND TRUCK & BUS PRODUCTION

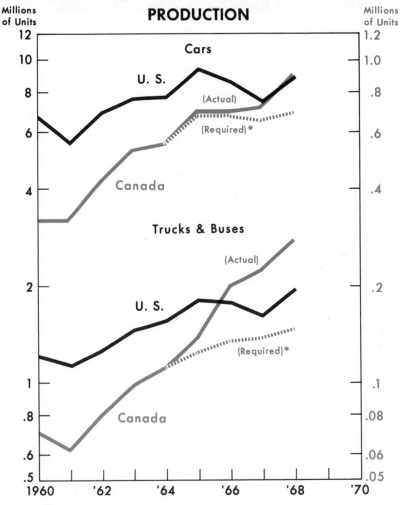

Source: Table 16
*See text for explanation

Chart 3

TOTAL NORTH AMERICAN VEHICLE PRODUCTION

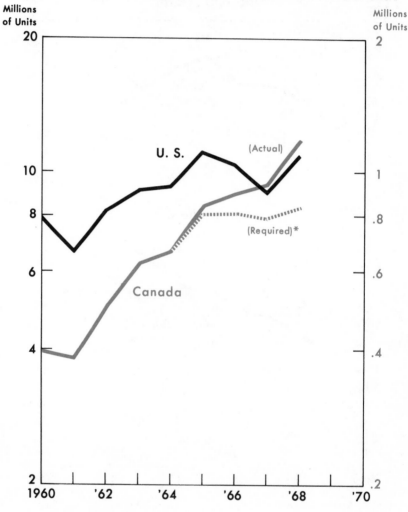

Source: Table 16

*See text for explanation

examine employment in the automotive industries as an alternative measure of production shares.[8]

Table 17 presents employment statistics for the years 1963 to 1968. Chart 4 plots these statistics, again using a vertical scale which is ten times greater for Canada than for the United States. Total automotive employment is broken into two reasonably comparable groupings, parts and accessories employees and others, mainly workers in vehicle assembly and body operations.

TABLE 17

ANNUAL AVERAGE EMPLOYMENT IN AUTOMOTIVE INDUSTRIES, 1963-68
(thousand employees)

Calendar Year	United States	Canada	Total	Canada's Share of Total (%)
Total Automotive				
1963	741.3	60.3	801.6	7.52
1964	752.9	69.3	822.2	8.43
1965	842.7	80.0	922.7	8.67
1966	861.6	84.9	946.5	8.97
1967	815.9	84.1	900.0	9.34
1968	867.8	83.4	951.2	8.77
Parts and Accessories				
1963	326.9	26.1	353.0	7.39
1964	336.7	30.5	367.2	8.31
1965	362.8	34.6	397.4	8.71
1966	370.2	38.8	409.0	9.49
1967	352.8	37.1	389.9	9.52
1968	377.0	35.4	412.4	8.58
Other (mainly assembly and bodies)				
1963	414.4	34.2	448.6	7.62
1964	416.2	38.8	455.0	8.53
1965	479.9	45.4	525.3	8.64
1966	491.4	46.1	537.5	8.58
1967	463.1	47.0	510.1	9.21
1968	490.8	48.0	538.8	8.91

Source: *Second Annual Report of the President to the Congress on the Operation of the Automotive Products Trade Act of 1965* (Washington: Government Printing Office, 1968), pp. 43-44. Also *Third Annual Report . . .*, 1969, p. 18.

The most interesting fact to emerge from these statistics is that Canada's share of automotive employment was only a little greater in 1968 than in 1964. After rising steadily between 1963 and 1967, the

---

[8]A change in the Standard Industrial Classification used in the United States has resulted in the grouping of vehicle production with parts and accessories production under a single heading.

Chart 4
AVERAGE ANNUAL AUTOMOTIVE EMPLOYMENT

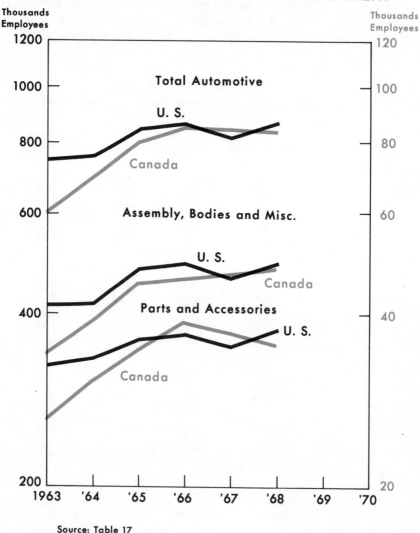

Source: Table 17

Canadian share declined rather significantly in 1968.[9] The chief factor accounting for this decline was a reduction in the number of Canadian employees engaged in parts and accessories production after 1966. Employment in other automotive activities in Canada has continued to expand, but by substantially less than what might have been anticipated on the basis of the increase in Canada's share of vehicle production in North America.

At this point we will anticipate the results of the next section, which demonstrates that Canada's share of total automotive activity has increased considerably since the 1965 Agreement. This fact, combined with the evidence on employment trends in this section, provides the basis for the following important conclusion:

The Automotive Agreement has, to date, been of primary stimulus to the level of Canadian output rather than to the level of Canadian employment. Put another way, the Agreement has not caused a marked shift of jobs away from the United States to Canada but has instead made the Canadian segment of the automotive labour force considerably more efficient.

C. Changes in the Automotive Trade Balance

We now come to the issue that has generated the greatest controversy during the life of the Agreement. On one point there is no doubt: the United States has experienced a substantial decline in its traditional automotive trade surplus with Canada following the Agreement. Attempts to measure the amount of the decline, however, have produced exceptionally large differences.

The extent of the problem is demonstrated by examining columns I and II in Table 18. Column I measures the U.S. trade balance for the period 1964-68 as reported in U.S. statistics, while column II measures it as reported in Canadian statistics (Canadian imports equal U.S. exports; Canadian exports equal U.S. imports). Whereas U.S. statistics show a deterioration of almost $740 million in the U.S. balance over the four years, the Canadian statistics show a decline of only about $190 million.[10] The discrepancy amounts to $550 million.

A detailed discussion of the reasons for these differences is left for a separate appendix (E) in Part IV of this study. We can summarize this discussion here by noting that there are two basic corrections which must be made in the statistics if we are to obtain an accurate picture of changes in the automotive trade balance.[11]

---

[9]To some extent this decline was due to labour disputes in Canada during 1968. When employment comparisons are based on a single month, November, which was not affected by strikes in Canada, Canada's share of the total is still shown to have declined, but the share of workers in the "other" category rose from the 1967 level.
[10]In this section all values are expressed in terms of U.S. dollars.

The first correction is to use Canadian parts imports as a measure of U.S. parts exports. Since certain parts can be used for a number of purposes (e.g., electrical components), it is difficult for officials in the exporting country to establish appropriate classifications. If the part is to be imported duty-free under the Agreement, however, it must be declared as an automotive product to officials in the importing country. Therefore, parts classifications, and thus statistics on automotive-parts trade, are more accurate in the importing country and, of relevance here, show larger reported volumes of trade.

TABLE 18

MEASURES OF THE UNITED STATES' AUTOMOTIVE
TRADE BALANCE WITH CANADA, 1964-68
(million dollars U.S.)

Calendar Year	I	II	III	IV
1964	+ 578.2	+ 569.0	+ 583.4	+ 564.4
1965	+ 613.1	+ 717.6	+ 682.4	+ 647.5
1966	+ 422.3	+ 601.6	+ 526.8	+ 531.9
1967	+ 239.2	+ 477.3	+ 439.1	+ 336.5
1968	− 159.3	+ 382.0	+ 164.0	+ 160.7
Change, 1964 to 1968	− 737.5	− 187.0	− 419.4	− 403.7
Basis for Measuring				
U.S. exports equal:	U.S. exports	Canadian imports	Canadian imports	U.S. exports
U.S. imports equal:	U.S. imports	Canadian exports	U.S. imports	Canadian imports

Source: See Appendix E, Table E-1.

Adopting this logic, the U.S. Administration has argued that Canadian import figures should be used to measure *all* U.S. automotive exports.[12] The result of this exercise is shown in column III of Table 18. On this basis the U.S. trade balance declined by about $420 million between 1964 and 1968. (An export-export balance, with Canadian exports used to measure U.S. imports, is also shown as column IV, for comparison. The decline in the U.S. balance on this basis was about $405 million.)

We find little justification for the U.S. Administration's argument for combining both countries' import data in the case of vehicle trade, since there could hardly be any doubt as to whether or not a car or a truck should be classified as an automotive product. For reasons outlined in Appendix E, the substantial discrepancy in the statistics on vehicle trade is resolved by using Canadian exports to measure U.S. imports in the vehicle categories (while accepting the combined import technique for parts). The rationale for this correction is that it more accurately reflects the value of vehicle trade as determined by the manufacturer's

[11]The term "automotive trade balance" should be stressed. Our interest here is in production shares in automotive products only. Another objective would require different measure of the balance (see Chapter 9).

[12]*Second Annual Report . . ., op. cit.,* p. 19.

own transaction prices rather than by essentially arbitrary (in this case) customs procedures.

Table 19 presents our best estimate of what has actually happened to the U.S. balance on automotive trade with Canada since 1964. Canadian parts imports are used to measure U.S. parts exports, and Canadian vehicle exports replace U.S. vehicle-import figures. As a result of these corrections, the U.S. trade surplus is shown to have declined by $357 million in the period 1964 to 1968.

Table 19 and Chart 5 show that the decline in the U.S. surplus since the Agreement has been due to the fact the United States has changed its position from that of a small net exporter of completed vehicles and chassis to that of a very large net importer of these products. The U.S. role as a net supplier of parts to Canada, on the other hand, has increased substantially during the years the Agreement has been in effect.

TABLE 19

BEST ESTIMATE[a] OF U.S. AUTOMOTIVE TRADE WITH CANADA,
BY PRODUCT CATEGORY, 1964-68
(million dollars U.S.)

Calendar Year	U.S. Exports	U.S. Imports	Balance
Total Automotive			
1964	659.6	73.3	+586.3
1965	931.1	221.0	+710.1
1966	1,397.1	817.6	+579.5
1967	1,955.6	1,503.1	+452.5
1968	2,586.2	2,356.5	+229.7
Change: 1964-68	+1,926.6	+2,283.2	−356.6
Cars			
1964	45.4	19.3	+ 26.1
1965	114.0	61.4	+ 52.6
1966	275.6	322.1	− 46.5
1967	563.0	760.3	− 197.3
1968	703.6	1,174.5	− 470.9
Change: 1964-68	+ 658.2	+1,155.2	−497.0
Trucks, Buses, Chassis			
1964	17.1	4.7	+ 12.4
1965	45.4	20.4	+ 25.0
1966	83.6	135.3	− 51.7
1967	138.3	268.7	− 130.4
1968	166.6	399.0	− 232.4
Change: 1964-68	+ 149.5	+ 394.3	−244.8
Parts and Accessories			
1964	597.1	49.3	+547.8
1965	771.7	139.2	+632.5
1966[b]	1,037.9	360.2	+677.7
1967	1,254.3	474.1	+780.2
1968	1,716.0	783.0	+933.0
Change: 1964-68	+1,118.9	+ 733.7	+385.2

[a]Estimate based upon import-import statistics for parts and export-export statistics for vehicles.
[b]Not strictly comparable with earlier years.
Source: See Appendix E, Table E-1.

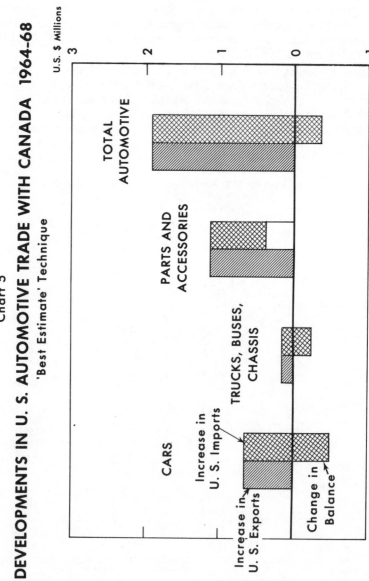

Chart 5

DEVELOPMENTS IN U. S. AUTOMOTIVE TRADE WITH CANADA 1964-68

'Best Estimate' Technique

Source: Table 19

The over-all U.S. automotive trade balance with Canada provides a reasonably exact measure of the size of the production-sales gap in Canada that was discussed in the introductory paragraphs of this section. Because the U.S. surplus has declined, we know that the value of Canadian automotive production has increased more rapidly than the value of Canadian purchases of North American-produced automotive products. Thus, the absolute size of the gap has narrowed, and as of 1968 it was only $230 million, compared with $587 million in 1964, just prior to the Agreement.[13]

The following conclusions can be drawn from the results that have been derived in this section:

1) The large increases in U.S. exports and imports of automotive products to and from Canada reflect the greatly expanded integration of production between the two countries resulting from the Agreement.

2) As bilateral trade flows have expanded in a gross sense, the *net* U.S. automotive trade surplus with Canada has declined by about $357 million between 1964 and 1968.

3) In order to account for the decline in the U.S. surplus, it was necessary for the value of Canadian automotive production to expand by an amount equal to $357 million *in addition to the full value of the growth of Canadian purchases of North American-produced vehicles,* thereby narrowing the production-sales gap in Canada markedly.

4) One of the "costs" of the Agreement to the U.S. automotive industry has therefore been that there was no *net* growth in sales to Canada between 1964 and 1968, but rather a decline in net sales equal to the reduction in the U.S. automotive trade surplus, or about $357 million.

D. Performance in Relation to the Commitments

On the basis of the results presented in this chapter, it is apparent that vehicle-manufacturers, in the aggregate, have exceeded the requirements placed upon them by the Canadian government.[14] Let us review performance in relation to each of the conditions in turn.

1. Production-to-Sales Ratio for Vehicles

The Agreement commits each manufacturer to maintain the ratio between the value of Canadian-assembled vehicles to the sales of vehicles

---

[13]By equating the size of the gap to the size of the U.S. trade surplus with Canada, we are neglecting Canadian production for export to third countries. We consider this factor in the following section.
[14]See Chapter 4 for a detailed discussion of these requirements.

in Canada at a level at least as great as in 1964.[15] Table 19 shows that Canada has become a large net exporter of completed vehicles to the United States, whereas in 1964 trade in vehicles was nearly balanced. We can therefore conclude that this condition has been met with a wide margin to spare.[16]

2. Canadian Value Added in Canadian-Produced Vehicles

The Agreement also requires that for those vehicles produced in Canada, the dollar amount of value added in Canada (Canadian content) was to be maintained at the level that was obtained in the 1964 model year. We conclude that this condition has been met on the basis of computations shown in Table 20.

First, in Appendix F in Part IV of this study we estimate that the value of Canadian vehicle sales, in terms of factory cost, increased by roughly U.S.$480 million between 1964 and 1968 (line 1, Table 20). *Second,* we add to this the Canadian production required to account for the change in the U.S. trade balance on complete vehicle trade with Canada, which is equal to about U.S.$740 million (line 2). The sum is then U.S.$1,220 million (line 3), which represents the 1964-68 growth in the value of Canadian vehicle production. *Third,* we must subtract from this the increase in total U.S. parts exports to Canada which were incorporated into this production, amounting to no more than U.S.$1,200 million over 1964-68 (line 4).[17] The resulting difference, U.S.$100 million (line 5), is the increase in Canadian value added in Canadian-produced vehicles. So, the condition to maintain the 1964 level of Canadian content was certainly achieved.[18]

3. Growth in Total Canadian Value Added

The letters of undertaking with the Canadian government committed vehicle-producers to increase Canadian value added at the end of the 1968 model year by U.S.$241 million (the equivalent of Can.$260 million) over that of the 1964 model year, plus 60 percent of the growth in their

[15]Technically, the 1964 model year was the base. However, since there was almost no difference in Canadian production and Canadian trade on a model-year and a calendar basis that year, we will continue to use calendar-year data, which are more readily available.
[16]It was possible for this condition to be met and still have Canada showing a net vehicle-trade deficit with the United States, provided Canadian exports to third countries increased sufficiently. This factor has been omitted for simplification.
[17]We are using here the amount of U.S. parts exports as measured by Canadian import statistics. Some replacement-parts trade is included in these statistics, so the estimate of the increase in Canadian content we come up with is understated to some extent, although the difference is small and on the order of $10 million.
[18]Again, exports to third countries, which strengthen the conclusion, have been omitted.

TABLE 20

GROWTH IN CANADIAN CONTENT IN CANADIAN-PRODUCED VEHICLES, 1964-68

Item		Amount (mil. $ U.S.)	Source
Line 1	Growth in the value of Canadian vehicle sales	480	Appendix E
Line 2	Increase in U.S. net imports of vehicles from Canada	740	Table 19
Line 3	Growth in gross value of Canadian vehicle production	1,220	Line 1 plus Line 2
Line 4	Increase in U.S. net exports of parts to Canada	1,120	Table 19
Line 5	Growth in Canadian content in Canadian vehicle production	100	Line 3 minus Line 4

Canadian car sales and 50 percent of the growth in their Canadian commercial vehicle sales. The calculations in Table 21 lead to the conclusion that by 1968 this total growth commitment was exceeded by a margin of about U.S.$396 million, or roughly one and two-thirds times the U.S.$241 million fixed commitment.

Table 21 takes into account the fact that, apart from the U.S.$241 million minimum growth that was promised to Canada, U.S. net exports to Canada could increase on two counts. *First*, as vehicle sales in Canada increased, a portion of the growth could be supplied from the United States (lines 1 through 5 in Table 21). In total, the sales growth that we estimate in Appendix F to have taken place in Canada would have permitted U.S. net exports to expand by U.S.$203 million as of 1968 (line 6). *Second*, as Canadian exports to third countries increased, there could be a matching increase in U.S. net exports to Canada, provided third-country imports by Canadian manufacturers subject to the Agreement did not increase as well. As is shown in Table 22, Canada increased its total automotive exports outside North America by U.S.$105 million between 1964 and 1968. From this, however, we subtract the U.S.$18 million increase in parts imports from third countries, leaving a total of U.S.$77 million (line 7, Table 21).[19]

---

[19]This is an approximation at best. What we are assuming is that all of the increase in Canadian parts imports from third countries during this period was for the purpose of using them as original equipment in the vehicles produced by manufacturers subject to the Agreement. To the extent that this is an overstatement, the estimate of the excess Canadian production above what was required to meet the conditions in the letters of undertaking (line 12, Table 21) is too low. On the other hand, some of the vehicles imported into Canada from third countries may have been accounted for by direct purchases from overseas affiliates of the Canadian producers. This fact tends to bias our estimate of excess Canadian production upward. We believe, however, that the bias is relatively minor.

The combination of these two factors would have allowed the U.S. automotive trade balance with Canada to increase by U.S.$280 million as of 1968 (line 8). From this amount must now be subtracted the U.S.$241 million fixed commitment in the letters of undertaking (line 9), leaving a maximum potential gain for the United States of U.S.$39 million (line 10). But as we have seen, the United States experienced a decline in its automotive trade balance with Canada of U.S.$357 million between 1964 and 1968 (line 11). (See Table 19.) Thus, the difference between what might have happened to the U.S. trade balance as a result of the

TABLE 21

GROWTH IN CANADIAN PRODUCTION IN EXCESS OF THE
COMMITMENTS IN THE LETTERS OF UNDERTAKING

	Item	Amount	Source
Line 1	Growth in the value of Canadian car sales, 1964-68	Can.$395 million	Appendix B
Line 2	Allowable increase in U.S. net exports as a result of Canadian car sales growth	Can.$158 million	40 percent of Line 1
Line 3	Growth in the value of Canadian commercial vehicle sales, 1964-68	Can.$125 million	Appendix B
Line 4	Allowable increase in U.S. net exports as a result of Canadian commercial vehicle sales growth	Can.$62 million	50 percent of Line 3
Line 5	Total allowable increase in U.S. net exports as a result of Canadian vehicle sales growth	Can.$220 million	Line 2 plus Line 4
Line 6	U.S. dollar equivalent of Line 5	U.S.$203 million	Line 5 times 0.925
Line 7	Increase in total Canadian automotive exports minus increase in Canadian parts imports, in trade with third countries, 1964-68	U.S.$77 million	Table 22
Line 8	Total allowable increase in U.S. net exports to Canada	U.S.$280 million	Line 6 plus Line 7
Line 9	Growth commitments in the letters of undertaking	U.S.$241 million	
Line 10	Maximum possible improvement in U.S. net exports to Canada, 1968	U.S.$39 million	Line 8 minus Line 9
Line 11	Actual decline in U.S. net exports to Canada, 1964-68	U.S.$357 million	Table 19
Line 12	Growth in Canadian production in excess of that needed to fulfill letters of undertaking	U.S.$396 million	Line 10 plus Line 11

TABLE 22

CANADIAN AUTOMOTIVE TRADE WITH COUNTRIES OTHER THAN THE UNITED STATES
(millions dollars U.S.)

Calendar Year	Exports	Imports	Balance
Total Automotive			
1964	75.5	109.2	− 33.7
1965	116.5	129.3	− 12.8
1966	141.8	116.7	+ 25.1
1967	136.5	130.9	+ 5.6
1968	181.0	211.6	− 30.6
Change: 1964-68	+ 105.5	+ 102.4	+ 2.9
Passenger Cars			
1964	43.4	87.5	− 44.1
1965	76.5	104.8	− 28.3
1966	75.4	88.5	− 13.1
1967	53.1	94.5	− 41.4
1968	80.7	155.1	− 74.4
Change: 1964-68	+ 37.3	+ 67.6	− 30.3
Trucks and Buses			
1964	8.3	2.0	+ 6.3
1965	9.3	1.9	+ 7.4
1966	24.6	2.4	+ 22.2
1967	32.5	2.6	+ 29.9
1968	41.6	8.5	+ 33.1
Change: 1964-68	+ 33.3	+ 6.5	+ 26.8
Parts and Accessories			
1964	23.8	19.7	+ 4.1
1965	30.7	22.6	+ 8.1
1966	41.8	25.9	+ 15.9
1967	50.8	33.7	+ 17.1
1968	58.7	48.1	+ 10.6
Change: 1964-68	+ 34.9	+ 28.4	+ 6.5

Source: *Second Annual Report of the President to the Congress on the Operation of the Automotive Products Trade Act of 1965* (Washington: Government Printing Office, 1968), p. 59. Also, *Third Annual Report . . .,* 1969, p. 26.

letters of undertaking alone and what actually took place between 1964 and 1968 is U.S.$396 million (line 12).

There should be no illusions about the exactness of the above calculations. In the absence of clear and complete statistics we have been forced to rely upon ingenuity, which always suggests the need for caution. But given this constraint, the results are significant enough to justify the following question: Why has Canada been able to achieve so much more as a result of the Agreement than would have been required to meet the various limitations on complete free trade? Some answers are provided in the next part of this study, along with some of their implications for the future.

Part III:
EVALUATION AND OUTLOOK

8

Why Have the Growth Commitments Been Exceeded?

Question: "What effect do we expect the Agreement and the companies' letters to have on the United States-Canadian balance of trade in automotive products in the next three years?"

Answer: "The Executive Branch agencies that have studied the problem carefully believe the *net surplus* of U.S. trade in automotive products with Canada through model year 1968 will remain firm at about the level of model years 1963-64, about $495 million to $580 million. It is estimated that there will be no substantial gain or loss in the present substantial U.S. surplus."[1]

Answer: "It is our expectation the program [the Agreement] will arrest the continuing growth of the unfavourable balance of trade and assure that it is maintained at about the present level; that is, in absolute dollars, something in the order of $500 million or $550 million."[2]

---

[1]Statement prepared by the U.S. Departments of State, Commerce, and Labor, May, 1965; see *Hearings on H.R. 9042 . . ., op. cit.,* p. 74.

[2]Canada's then Minister of Industry Drury as reported in *House of Commons Debates,* May 10, 1965, p. 1131, as cited in *ibid.,* p. 75. This is a short-term prediction. Canada's view of the longer-term outlook was probably better reflected in Drury's statement upon the Agreement's signing (Ottawa, January 15, 1965): "The program will make an important contribution to the improvement of Canada's international payments position. In recent years trade in vehicles and components has resulted in an annual deficit with the United States of the magnitude of $600 million. Increased output and improved efficiency in the automotive industries will help to achieve the Government's objective of reducing Canada's current account deficit."

As the above quotations indicate, both sides publicly predicted that the Agreement would cause no marked change in the automotive trade balance. They were wrong. In part the error lay in an optimistic projection of the growth in Canadian vehicle sales during the period 1965 to 1968. We have tried to adjust for this factor in Chapter 7, but we still come up with the conclusion that while the U.S. trade surplus declined by about $357 million between calendar 1964 and 1968, the growth commitments placed on the manufacturers could have been met with the U.S. surplus showing a decline of only about $38 million.[3] Our purpose in this chapter is to explore possible explanations for this development which so dramatically contradicts the forecast trade effects. These include definitional problems related to the commitments, the manufacturers' desire to surpass them by considerable safety margins, "lumpiness" in the addition of production facilities, and the disappearance of Canada's relative cost disadvantage in automotive production.

A. Possible Reasons for Overfulfillment

1. Canada's Definition of the Factory Cost of Imported Vehicles

The letters of undertaking committed the manufacturers to expand value added in Canada by a percentage (60 percent for cars and 50 percent for trucks) of the increase in the factory cost of their vehicle sales in Canada. In our calculation of the excess growth in Canadian value added (Table 21, Chapter 7), we assumed — as did, apparently, those who forecast little change in the U.S. trade balance — that the remaining increase in the value of vehicle sales in Canada could be supplied by net exports from the United States. Because of the method Canada seems to have adopted for valuing imported vehicles, however, the possibilities for expanding net U.S. exports were to some extent illusory.

We can illustrate this point with a simple example. Suppose that prior to the Agreement a car was produced in Canada at a factory cost of $1,800. Following the Agreement a decision was made to source this car from the United States at an intracompany transfer price of $2,000.[4] For purposes of determining the obligations of the manufacturers within the letters of undertaking, Canada has treated such a shift as leading to

---

[3]The $38 million figure is obtained by subtracting line 5 from line 9 in Table 21, Chapter 7. In this chapter all values are expressed in U.S. dollar equivalents.
[4]For purposes of valuing vehicle imports for official Canadian trade statistics, U.S. dealers' prices, which are higher than intracompany transfer prices, have been used (see Table E.2, Appendix E).

a $200 increase in the cost of vehicles sold in Canada, even though the number of vehicles sold was unchanged.[5]

Because of our treatment of the sales-growth factor (Table 21), we would estimate that U.S. net exports to Canada could have increased by $80 as a result of this hypothetical shift in production location (0.4 times $200). But this was not the case at all. Quite to the contrary, *Canadian* net exports would have to expand by $120 (0.6 times $200) in order to meet the requirements in the letters.[6] In other words, we have overstated the chances for increasing U.S. net exports by $200 ($80 + $120), or by the difference between the intracompany transfer price and factory cost in Canada.

We have omitted this problem of valuation procedures from our original estimate of the extent to which manufacturers exceeded their growth commitments because precise estimates are impossible to obtain. We can establish potential orders of magnitude, however, by referring to Table F-1, Appendix F (see Part IV). Since Canada imported about 347,000 more vehicles from the United States in 1968 than in 1964 (line 4 minus line 1, Table F-1), a difference of $100 between per vehicle factory cost in Canada and the price of imports for the purpose of determining the value-added growth commitments reduces our estimate of the overfulfillment by $34.7 million.

The point behind this rather complicated discussion is an important one. A portion of the apparent excess in the growth of Canadian value added was due to a valuation procedure in Canada which added another dimension to the growth commitments in the letters of undertaking. With intracompany transfer prices rather than factory costs being used to value Canadian vehicle imports, a decision to source a vehicle sold in Canada from the United States raised the amount of value added required of the Canadian vehicle-producer. Still, our original estimate of the overfulfillment by the manufacturers in 1968 — $396 million (line 12, Table 21) — is considerably more than can possibly be explained by this factor alone, although a difference of as much as $500 per vehicle between the Cana-

---

[5] In a letter to the Canadian government from Mr. Karl E. Scott, president of Ford Motor Company of Canada, Limited, on January 14, 1965, a concern was expressed that U.S. dealers' prices would be the basis for determining the "cost" of imported vehicles. See Committee on Finance, *op. cit.,* pp. 50-51. Conversations with one of the manufacturers, however, indicated that intracompany transfer prices have been used; as a general principle these are lower than dealers' prices by the amount of the markup allowed for distribution (over) margins, but higher than factory cost by the amount of the markup for manufacturing and assembly margins.

[6] With the car being assembled in Canada, $1,200 (0.6 times $2,000) in Canadian content had to be achieved in order to avoid all duties on the sale. By shipping the car from the United States, $1,320 (0.6 times $2,200) in Canadian value added had to be produced to meet the commitments in the letters. The difference, $120, was the amount by which net exports from Canada had to increase (or net imports to Canada had to fall).

dian factory cost and the intracompany transfer price would reduce the estimated excess by almost $175 million.[7]

2. Manufacturers' Safety Margins

Automobile sales exhibit a cyclical pattern over time which is difficult to forecast in advance. As the manufacturers approached the task of meeting their commitments to the Canadian government, a key factor in their decisions was the need to allow an adequate safety margin in the event that market forces lowered Canadian production or raised Canadian sales from projected levels. What made this an essential policy, rather than merely a prudent one, was the design of the commitments. The penalties for non-fulfillment confronted the producers with an all-or-nothing situation and the prospect of paying duties on all their automotive imports on the basis of the old tariff structure (described in Chapter 1).

There is no reason to doubt that the need for a safety margin was an essential factor behind the overfulfillment of the commitments. What we would question is whether this factor, plus the above-mentioned Canadian method for determining growth in factory costs, could possibly account for all the overfulfillment that we originally estimated. To the extent that production costs in Canada remained higher than in the United States, maintaining such a safety margin would, after all, have entailed a burden for the producers. Therefore, while we accept that safety margins may have been responsible for part of the unexpectedly large decline in the U.S. trade balance, it is likely that two other factors, to which we now turn, must have been present as well.

3. "Lumpiness" in Additions to Production Facilities

As we discussed in Chapter 1, the automotive industry is subject to significant economies of scale. Indeed, the inability to achieve full advantage from these economies through production of a diversified range of products for a small home market was the main factor behind Canada's unilateral efforts to encourage Canadian production for export markets. Given the fact that some expansion of their Canadian operations would be necessary to meet the growth requirements in the letters of undertaking, the vehicle-producers undoubtedly decided to plan these facilities to take full advantage of scale economies.

Three considerations support the argument that the decline in the U.S. automotive trade balance was to a large extent due to the lumpy growth of automotive production facilities, with the major recent lumps occurring in Canada:

---

[7]It was shown above that a difference of $100 per vehicle would produce a reduction of $34.7 million, so five times this amount is $173.5 million.

1)   So long as per unit costs declined sufficiently with increases in planned capacity, any burden in carrying an adequate safety margin was reduced.

2)   While the output of an optimal-sized assembly plant might be small in comparison with the U.S. market, it is necessary to consider that the Canadian operations of the producers were only about one-tenth as large as in the United States. The output of an additional plant in Canada of optimal design could, therefore, cause a very significant impact on Canada's balance of trade with the United States.

3)   Basic investment decisions for expanding Canadian facilities were made in 1965, a year in which vehicle sales in North America reached a pronounced peak. If a firm required additional capacity, the decision to expand at one location in Canada may have been superior to building in both Canada and the United States or, alternatively, operating at levels above planned capacity in existing U.S. plants.

It will be noted from Table 19 in Chapter 7 that the biggest decline in the U.S. trade balance came in 1968, a year in which North American vehicle sales again reached a cyclical peak. The "lumpiness" argument would suggest that the large increase in Canadian output that year arose because capacity for expanding was there at lower cost than would be possible from existing plants in the United States. The reasoning is quite plausible, and it may go a long way towards explaining why the predictions about the U.S. automotive trade balance turned out to be wrong. But we are not convinced that we have as yet exhausted all the possibilities.

4. Disappearance of Canada's Relative Cost Disadvantage

Every analysis of the probable impact of the Agreement on the U.S. automotive trade balance with which we are familiar was based on the assumption — rarely stated explicitly — that production costs in Canada would remain above those in the United States at least through the 1968 model year. In fact, this assumption provided one of the basic rationales for Canada's insistence upon the various constraints upon complete free trade which were contained in the Agreement and the letters of under-taking. Our analysis leads us to the conclusion that the validity of this assumption should be challenged.

The three explanations for the estimated $396 million overfulfillment of the growth commitments which we have discussed to this point are plausible reasons why production in Canada might have grown by more than had been anticipated even if costs were higher there than in the United States. But if these three factors did not add up to an amount nearly as great as the overfulfillment, the only other explanation must be that the vehicle-manufacturers, in the aggregate, have acted as if Canadian production costs have been reduced to a point where they are no greater than in the United States for a substantial volume of output. And if this hypothesis is accepted, the safety margin and "lumpiness" arguments lose some of their status as primary causes.[8]

For which products does it appear most likely that production costs in Canada have come down at least to U.S. levels? In the case of vehicle assembly we cannot be sure, since, as we have shown in Section C of Chapter 6, the vehicle-manufacturers adopted the strategy of meeting a significant portion of their minimum growth commitments by expanding their assembly operations in Canada. The "lumpiness" explanation enters at this point and precludes us from asserting positively that Canadian assembly would not have grown as rapidly if production costs at a particular volume of output were somewhat higher in Canada than in the United States.

The production of parts and accessories is a different matter. Once a reasonable safety margin was assured by their assembly activities, there was no reason for the manufacturers to bear excess costs on parts exports from Canada to the United States. Nor can the "lumpiness" argument be appealed to, since, as Table 15 in Chapter 5 demonstrates, increases in a great variety of parts exports have been achieved, and between 1964 and 1968 Canadian exports of parts and accessories to the United States expanded by $734 million in total (see Table 19, Chapter 7). Unless parts exports could be sourced as cheaply in Canada as in the United States, our findings indicate that a very ample margin existed for the transfer of production from Canada.

The path we have taken to reach this conclusion has been, of necessity, a circuitous one. If the statistics had been available, a direct comparison of production costs in the two countries would certainly be the preferred course.[9] We have been constrained to work with the data at hand, however, and on the basis of our reading of these data it is probable that one of the major reasons for the overfulfillment of the growth commitments is that it has not been particularly costly for the firms to do so.

---

[8]Note, again, that the safety margin and "lumpiness" factors are not strictly additive: "lumpiness" produces a built-in safety margin.

[9]Manufacturing statistics comparable to those discussed in Chapter 3 will soon be available for 1968, but there will be a number of problems in interpreting them. Chief among these will be to obtain fairly exact estimates of the value of capital per worker now that barriers to integrated production have been sharply reduced. Furthermore, it is possible for *average* production costs to remain higher in Canada because of remaining restrictions on free trade, while costs on increments to Canadian output are about the same as, or less than, in the United States.

Even if this hypothesis is rejected, the discussion of comparative production costs focuses our attention on the factor that will have the most significant impact on the operation of the Agreement in the years ahead. But before we elaborate upon this point, let us first turn to the question of where the Agreement stands at present, more than a year and a half after the end of the 1968 model year (July 31, 1968), by which time the manufacturers had to meet the Can.$260 million fixed growth commitments in their letters of undertaking.

B. Has the Agreement Entered a New Phase?

In accordance with the provisions of the Agreement, on December 13, 1967, a joint governmental review of its operation was begun. On September 4, 1968, President Johnson issued a special report on this review which said, in effect, that the study had been completed and further consultations would take place later.[10] The only item of significance contained in this report was the assurance that no additional undertakings to increase Canadian value added had been made by the manufacturers.[11]

Where, then, does this leave the status of the Agreement? In most respects, nothing has changed.

1) Manufacturers are still the only ones able to obtain duty-free imports in Canada.

2) To qualify as a Canadian manufacturer, a firm must still achieve at least the same vehicle production-to-sales ratio in Canada as in the 1964 model year.

3) In addition, the firm must still achieve at least the same absolute amount of Canadian content in Canadian vehicle production as in the 1964 model year.

4) Finally, the vehicle-manufacturers must still increase Canadian value added by a percentage (60 percent for cars and 50 percent for commercial vehicles) of the increase in their vehicle sales in Canada.[12]

In one important area there has been a change, however, and this may justify the assertion that a new phase has begun in the life of the Agreement: after the end of the 1968 model year the manufacturers were under no further obligation from their letters of undertaking to increase

---

[10]House of Representatives, Doc. No. 379, 90th Congress, 2nd Session. At the initiative of the U.S. State Department, the first such consultations were held in November, 1969, and sequels are scheduled as this study goes to press.

[11]*Ibid.*, p. 5.

[12]The first three conditions are written into the Agreement itself, which has not been changed. The fourth was in the original letters of undertaking; since no termination date was specified for this provision, we assume that it remains in effect.

Canadian value added beyond that required by the growth in Canadian vehicles sales.[13]

With the conditions in the Agreement and the letters of undertaking as they now stand, it is possible for the U.S. automotive trade balance with Canada to improve with growth in Canada's vehicle purchases. Specifically, net exports from the United States can increase by up to 40 percent of the growth in car sales and 50 percent of the growth in commercial vehicle sales in Canada. And if this occurs, the absolute size of the production-sales gap in Canada (as discussed in Chapter 7) will again increase.

Still incomplete statistics on developments during 1969 do not indicate such an occurrence, as would be signaled by a partial recovery of the U.S. trade balance. Indeed, as Table 23 shows, there was a further sharp deterioration in this balance over the first three quarters of 1969, and prospects are for a sizable deficit, no matter how measured, for 1969 as a whole.[14] This turn of events would be very curious indeed if production costs remain higher in Canada than in the United States. While it is conceivable that Canadian assembly continues to expand to achieve efficient utilization of facilities in place, any parts production at a higher cost in Canada should most certainly have been reduced during this period.

C. Conclusions

There are basically two possibilities as to the long-term outlook with the Agreement in its present form. On the one hand, production costs in Canada may reach a point — if they have not done so already — where the restrictions in the Agreement are irrelevant so far as the volume of Canadian automotive output is concerned. In other words, we would have nearly the same results that would hold under a free trade arrangement in the North American automotive industry. And in this event, there would be just as much reason to expect a deficit in the U.S. automotive trade balance with Canada as there would be to expect a surplus.

---

[13]There has been some doubt expressed about the current status of the Can.$260 million fixed growth commitment. Although this is really a question of how the Canadian government interprets the original letters, our assumption is that value-added growth related to sales growth in Canada must proceed from a base which is now Can.$260 million greater than the original 1964 model-year level.

[14]We do not think the results in Table 23 reflect the exact value of the balance in absolute terms for reasons discussed in Appendix E. Nevertheless, the direction and magnitude of the change are definitely meaningful. On the basis of past relationships between the balance on the transactions basis and our "best estimate" of the balance (export-export for vehicles, import-import for parts, see Table 19, Chapter 7), we estimate that a more exact measure of the U.S. trade deficit during the first three quarters of 1969 would be between $100 million and $150 million at an annual rate.

TABLE 23

U.S. AUTOMOTIVE TRADE WITH CANADA, 1968-69[a]
(million dollars U.S.)

| | First Three Quarters | | |
	1968	1969	Change
U.S. exports to Canada	2,316	2,813	+497
U.S. imports from Canada:			
Regular basis	2,424	3,356	+932
Transactions basis[b]	2,144	3,023	+879
U.S. balance:			
Regular basis	−108	−543	−435
Transactions basis[b]	+172	−210	−382

[a]All figures are expressed at seasonally adjusted annual rates.
[b]Prices used are said to be intracompany transfer prices supplied by the manufacturers.

Source: U.S. Department of Commerce, Office of Business Economics, *Survey of Current Business,* December, 1969, p. 30.

The alternative possibility is that production costs in Canada will generally tend to be higher than those in the United States in the long run.[15] As the Agreement now stands, higher costs in Canadian locations would mean an eventual return to a growing gap between production and sales there, with the automotive trade surplus of the United States again increasing in proportion to the expansion in Canadian vehicle purchases. The conditions in the Agreement and the original letters of undertaking would still set a limit on how large that surplus might be, but the reasons for overfulfillment of the commitments thus far — valuation methods, safety margins, and "lumpiness" — would tend merely to produce a gap that grows from a smaller base than otherwise.

As we have discussed in Chapter 4, predictions made back in 1965 about the costs and benefits of the Agreement to both countries were based on the implicit assumption that while integration of North American automotive production would increase efficiency in Canada, a Canadian cost disadvantage would remain. Therefore, it was concluded, limitations on free trade contained in the Agreement and the letters of undertaking would determine the maximum level of production that would take place in Canada. This was not a particularly sound basis for analysis at the time,

[15]To this point we have neglected the question of the effects of transport costs on the advantages of locating production in Canada. This factor may be relatively minor because virtually all automotive production facilities in Canada, with the exception of General Motors' assembly plant in Ste. Thérèse, Quebec, are within two hundred miles of Detroit. Still, to be strictly correct in our discussion it should be stressed that location in Canada will be preferred only if any transportation cost disadvantage there is more than offset by advantages in terms of other costs.

and the results of our investigation suggest that it is even less sound now that the Agreement has been in effect for some five years. In Chapter 9 we will re-examine the issues arising from the Agreement, taking into account the impact of developments in comparative production costs. Then, in Chapter 10, we will examine the implications of possible proposals for modifying and/or expanding the Automotive Agreement.

9

Re-examination of the Issues

In Chapter 5 we discussed the anticipated costs and benefits of the Agreement on the assumption that there would be little change in net U.S. automotive sales to Canada. Then, in Chapter 7, we demonstrated that net U.S. sales actually declined — by our "best estimate" — by about U.S.$357 million between 1964 and 1968 (see Table 19). Moreover, although the statistics are still incomplete, it appears that in 1969 alone there was a further decline by an amount that may have been as great as during the previous four years taken together (see Table 23). Despite this record, there has as yet been little serious opposition to the Agreement by American automotive workers or independent parts-producers, although it was these groups that stood to lose the most from the actual course of events.[1]

The lack of opposition among these groups can probably be explained by examining the production, employment, and trade statistics in Tables 16, 17, and 19 in Chapter 7. North American demand for vehicles during this period was so strong that over two million more units were produced in 1968 than in 1964 (Table 16). This growth so overshadowed the distributional impact of the Agreement that there were about 115,000 more Americans working in automotive industries during 1968 than during 1964, and 40,000 of the increase came in parts and accessories operations (Table 17). And even though net sales of all U.S. automotive products

---

[1]Because of time and data limitations we have not examined the impact of the Agreement on Canada's independent parts-manufacturers in any detail. These firms have, in general, achieved efficiency gains; but it does not appear that their share of North American automotive output has increased to any significant degree, and it may even be that it has declined. A study of both countries' independent parts-manufacturers might produce some interesting and important contrasts to our conclusions, which are based primarily on aggregative results.

108   THE CANADA-U.S. AUTOMOTIVE AGREEMENT

to Canada declined by U.S.$357 million between 1964 and 1968, net sales of parts and accessories to Canada increased by U.S.$385 million (Table 19). Therefore, throughout most of this period there were plentiful job opportunities and alternative sources of demand for workers and firms who might otherwise have been dislocated by the shift in North American automotive production shares that has taken place since the Agreement was put into effect.

The same point can be illustrated by the experience of the adjustment assistance program that was set up when the Agreement was enacted in the United States.[2] Through June 30, 1968, when the program expired, only twenty-one groups of workers and not a single firm had submitted petitions for assistance. Of the twenty-one petitions by workers' groups, fourteen were granted, making a total of about 2,500 employees eligible for payments under the program. Of these, 1,950 were actually out of work long enough to receive benefits.[3] These numbers represent roughly 0.3 percent of the 750,000 American workers employed in automotive plants during 1964 (Table 17).

Canada too had a program of assistance; and a comparison with the U.S. experience provides a good indication of the relative extent of restructuring that was necessary in the two countries. Through 1968, a total of 8,000 Canadian workers had been declared as eligible for benefits.[4] This represents 11.6 percent of the 69,000 workers in Canadian automotive plants during 1964 (Table 17). In addition, seventy loans amounting to U.S.$52 million had been authorized for Canadian firms requiring assistance to adjust to the impact of the Agreement.

Automotive sales in North America exhibit a cyclical pattern, and signs of a marked slump began to emerge in late 1969 and early 1970. If this slump continues, it could provide the first real test of U.S. reactions to the Agreement. The increased share of North American automotive production which Canada has been able to gain as a result of the Agreement will undoubtedly provoke more of a response among American automotive workers and independent parts-producers — and those who represent them in the union and in the Congress — in a period of lay-offs and absolute sales declines.

It would be a mistake to judge the costs and benefits of the Agreement solely on the basis of cyclical developments in the industry. The decline to date in net U.S. automotive sales to Canada did result in a lower rate of growth in jobs for American automotive workers, but positive growth was still possible because vehicle demand in the United States was so

[2]See *Third Annual Report . . ., op. cit.,* pp. 32-34.
[3]*Ibid.,* pp. 12-13.
[4]*Ibid.,* p. 13.

strong. If lay-offs of existing workers are now necessary, it will be primarily because this demand has slackened. Only if Canada's share of production relative to its share of consumption should continue to rise during this period could those laid off legitimately point to the Agreement as the cause. The most likely course of events will be that the number of workers employed in both countries will decline during the slump, and the outcome in terms of production shares will be determined chiefly by changes in demand for the particular vehicle models that the producers have chosen to concentrate on in their Canadian facilities.[5]

The main issues arising from the Agreement concern long-term effects, and it is virtually certain that once the temporary sales slump has passed, there will be a resumption of positive growth in production and employment in both countries' automotive industries. Still, the Agreement has led to noticeable changes in production shares, and the sales slump will serve to highlight this fact. As a result, chances are that a number of important economic issues will now be given a more careful analysis than at the time the original public predictions of the Agreement's effects were made.

The approach in this chapter will be to consider, first, what the basis for determining production shares in the future will be — market forces or continuing restrictions on free trade. Then, we will examine the relevance of wage rates and vehicle prices in Canada under either set of conditions, and we will follow this with a more detailed analysis of the balance of payments implications of changing production shares. The reasons for concentrating upon these topics and the interrelationships that exist among them will be clarified as we proceed.

A. Production Shares: The Result of Market Forces or Protection?

The objectives of the 1965 Automotive Agreement, as stated in Article I (see Appendix A in Part IV), are the following:

a) The creation of a broader market for automotive products within which the full benefits of specialization and large-scale production can be achieved;

b) The liberalization of United States and Canadian automotive trade in respect of tariff barriers and other factors tending to

---

[5]See Section C.1, Chapter 6. The level of Ford's Canadian production, for example, will depend upon developments in demand for Mavericks. Given enough time to adjust, assembly plants have almost complete flexibility in terms of the models that can be produced, but the costs involved in making temporary changes are high.

impede it, with a view to enabling the industries of both countries to participate on a fair and equitable basis in the expanding
total market of the two countries;

c) The development of conditions in which market forces may
operate effectively to attain the most economic pattern of investment, production and trade.

Before we can come to grips with the real issues arising from the
Agreement, it is essential that the meaning of this statement of objectives
be clarified. Just what have the two countries agreed to do?

Because of the use of such phrases as "full benefits of specialization
and large-scale production" and "most economic pattern of investment,
production and trade," the statement of objectives would appear to be a
prolix expression of commitment by Canada and the United States to free
trade in automotive products. We have seen in Chapter 4, however, that
the letters of undertaking placed a number of constraints on the operation
of "market forces." The stated rationale for these constraints was that
they were necessary to ensure that the Canadian automotive industry
would "participate on a fair and equitable basis in the expanding total
market of the two countries" during the period of transitional adjustments
to the Agreement.

On the basis of our analysis in Chapters 6 and 7, we conclude that,
for the most part, these transitional adjustments have been completed
and, to the extent that "market forces" have been permitted "to attain
the most economic pattern of investment, production and trade," Canada
has done quite well indeed. There is still a need for convincing proof of
how much adjustment remains to be done; but the point we want to concentrate upon here is that, for the goal of "enabling the industries of both
countries to participate on a fair and equitable basis in the expanding
total market of the two countries," Canada persists in defining "fair and
equitable" in terms of the size of the gap between Canadian production
and consumption of automotive products.[6]

By specifically committing the vehicle-producers to a total increase
in Canadian value added of Can.$260 million (Table 9) irrespective of
the growth in vehicle sales in Canada, the Canadian government ensured
that the relative size of the production-sales gap would be narrowed. But
after the 1968 model year ended on July 31, 1968, there was no longer

---

[6]One of the bluntest statements of a view that is widely shared in Canada appeared
in an editorial in the Toronto *Globe and Mail*, "Reassessing self-interest in
U.S.-Canada auto pact," on November 13, 1969. "As long as the Canadian-produced
share of [the North American] market remains considerably below our consumption,
the Canadian negotiators have a strong case to demand that our interests be
protected."

any assurance for Canada that this gap would not widen both absolutely and relatively (see Section B, Chapter 8). As a result, Canada has sought, unsuccessfully so far, to obtain additional production guarantees.[7]

The Canadian government has carefully avoided specifying any target relationship between production and sales shares that would signal that the time had come to remove all restrictions on free trade in automotive products. It is relevant, however, that in 1969 Canada's own automotive trade statistics, which have consistently shown the best U.S. position of any measure (see Table 18), may produce a Canadian surplus for the first time and proof that its share of production exceeds its share of consumption.[8]

The question of production guarantees for Canada is one of the key items being discussed in the current intergovernmental review of the Agreement. It is not our purpose to recommend what the objectives of Canada and the United States should be, although once the differences in approach have been resolved, it would help clarify the ambiguity about what the Agreement represents if rhetoric were made to conform with real purposes. Before we can continue with an analysis of the economic issues, however, it is necessary to make some assumption regarding the future status of these production guarantees. Based on past experience, there is a high probability that some guarantee will remain, even if it takes the form of an implicit recognition on the part of the producers that too low a level of production will provoke Canada to abrogate the Agreement. When it comes right down to basics, Canada is unwilling to permit the level of automotive activity there to be determined, in good times and bad, solely on the basis of decisions by firms whose head offices are located in the United States.[9]

---

[7]"Totally apart from the Agreement, the Canadian Government continues to persist in seeking higher Canadian content than the current requirements. Even if this results in higher automobile prices, they believe that the Canadian public would support such action to assure continued increase in Canadian automotive employment. To Canadians the subject of more extensive Canadian manufacture is not a theoretical concept, it is a matter of national pride." Statement by Brian T. O'Keefe, Chrysler Corp., *Canadian Automotive Agreement*, Hearing Before the Committee on Finance, United States Senate, 90th Congress, 2nd Session, July 19, 1968 (Washington: Government Printing Office, 1968), p. 46.

[8]For the first nine months of 1969 a deficit of about Can.$90 million with the U.S. was registered, compared with about Can.$320 million during the corresponding period in 1968. Canada's position on this measure has improved steadily in 1969, and a continuation of this trend during the last three months of the year could bring the yearly total into surplus. See DBS Cat. Nos. 65-002 and 65-005. Also see Table 23, Chapter 8.

[9]This point is probably not a real bone of contention with the United States government. The question that is being debated is whether the argument that U.S. parents might distort decisions based on market forces is being used as a pretence to force more production in Canada than true market forces would support.

If production guarantees to Canada, either explicit or implicit, are retained, the key question becomes how great these guarantees are relative to the amount of automotive production Canada could achieve under conditions of unrestricted free trade in these products. There are two possibilities: either the guarantees turn out to be redundant in the sense that Canada would be able to attain at least this level of production on the basis of comparative costs; or the guarantees cause total costs of North American automotive production to be excessive. We turn now to an analysis of the factors that will determine which of these two alternatives will be observed, once a particular guarantee has been determined.

B. The Significance of Wage "Parity" in Canada

The terms "market forces" and "most economic pattern of auto-motive production," contained in the statement of the Agreement's objectives, have very precise meanings in economics. Government pres-sures, market power of firms, and bargaining strength of unions are all factors that can prevent these goals from being achieved. Furthermore, so long as tariff and taxation differences exist in any sector that supplies inputs to the automotive industry — and this includes every sector, when we come right down to it — distortions from the most efficient pattern of production locations will remain. It is easy to see, therefore, that the most that can be hoped for from an *ad hoc,* single-sector approach to free trade is a reasonable approximation to the ideal objectives stated in the Automotive Agreement of 1965.

The relevance of all this to the question of production shares is that changes in a host of economic variables will affect the level of automotive output in Canada that can be supported on the basis of market forces. In this regard, one of the most significant developments that has occurred since the Agreement was signed came in 1967, when the United Automobile Workers obtained contracts from the "Big Three" producers that guaranteed that by September, 1970, Canadian workers will be paid the same dollar wage for the same job classification as U.S. workers. Since the Canadian dollar is worth only 0.925 of a U.S. dollar, this commitment amounts to nominal rather than real wage parity, but the distinction is rather secondary for our purposes. Of primary importance is the concept that wages in a particular industry in Canada should bear a relationship to U.S. wages in the same industry rather than conforming to the general wage level in Canada.

The difficulty in analyzing wage parity between Canada and the United States in a single sector is that it does not fit very neatly into the traditional model of economic behaviour based upon the primacy of competitive market forces.[10] In this model, the type of productivity gains achieved in the Canadian automotive industry as a result of the Agreement would not be translated into a wage boost in one industry alone. Rather, competitive pressures would tend to reduce prices of automotive products, leading to a growth in demand for these products; and finally, if demand grew sufficiently, the process of bidding additional workers into the industry might produce some upward movement in general money wage rates.[11] The basis for this chain of events lies in the model's assumption that free entry exists for both firms and factors of production, so eventually the payments for capital and labour employed in any industry will be no greater than their opportunity cost, which is determined in the market as a whole.

If the assumption of free entry does not hold, as in the case of the motor vehicle industry, this model breaks down: prices become a function of market power and wages a function of bargaining strength. The combination of a desire by existing Canadian automotive workers to achieve the highest wages possible plus the goal of American automotive workers to prevent a shift in production to Canada from threatening their job security created strong pressures on union management to close the gap in relative wages between the two sectors of the industry. Nominal wage parity seemed the obvious bargaining position to take.[12] At the same time, given the fact that the Agreement reduced the major barriers to equal efficiency in U.S. and Canadian operations, the vehicle-producers were not able to reject nominal wage parity very vigorously, especially since it would come gradually over three years and still leave the real wage rate in Canada about 7 percent below that in the United States.

If vehicle-producers and workers employed in the industry at a point in time were the only parties affected by wage parity, we would probably let the matter drop here. But this is certainly not the case. The real significance of the issue of relative automotive workers' wages can be seen by observing an important fact: If wage rates in the United States, transport charges, technology, and the comparative costs of all other factor inputs in both countries are fixed, the level of Canadian automotive production that would take place on the basis of market forces will be determined

---

[10]Wage parity with the United States has already been achieved or surpassed in a limited number of Canadian industries, including steel and forest products. The very same problem of explaining this wage pattern on the basis of a purely competitive market model arises there, although specific details differ.

[11]It would also be possible for money wage rates to fall if, for example, productivity increases were so great that fewer workers were required to produce the new level of output demanded. In any event, real wages would tend to rise to the extent that prices of the good in question fell.

[12]Obvious, that is, given the fact that both countries' currencies are called dollars and that near parity exists in the rate of exchange. An interesting set of problems would have had to be faced if Canada's currency was called, say, Canadian francs, trading at four to the U.S. dollar.

by the level of wages in Canada. The point to stress is this: Canada has expressed hopes of achieving at least a near balance between automotive production and automotive purchases there; the chances that this result might occur from the free operation of market forces are closely related to the level of wages that must be paid in Canada.

It will be recalled from Section A.4 of Chapter 8 that one of the reasons why the commitments of the manufacturers have been exceeded by a wide margin (Table 21) may be that production costs for a substantial volume of parts output in Canada have been reduced at least to U.S. levels. One reason for this could be the behaviour of average hourly earnings in Canada, as shown in Table 24.

TABLE 24

AVERAGE HOURLY EARNINGS IN CANADIAN AUTOMOTIVE INDUSTRIES, 1964-68
(Canadian dollars)

Year	Motor Vehicle Manufacturers (A)	Motor Vehicle Parts Manufacturers (B)	(A) − (B)
1964	2.68	2.47	0.21
1965	2.87	2.61	0.26
1966	2.94	2.65	0.29
1967	3.10	2.78	0.32
1968	3.49	3.03	0.46
Increase: 1964-68	0.81	0.56	0.25

Source: Dominion Bureau of Statistics, Cat. No. 72-202.

Wage parity has not been generally agreed to by Canadian parts-manufacturers, and average hourly earnings of the employees of these firms rose by Can.$0.56 between 1964 and 1968, while for vehicle-manufacturers the increase during the same period was Can.$0.81.[13] Although we cannot say that overfulfillment would definitely have been less if wages had risen by as much for parts-manufacturers as they did for vehicle-manufacturers, any future narrowing of wage differences between the two categories will certainly be a factor affecting Canada's share of production.

As we will discuss in the next section, vehicle prices remain higher in Canada than in the United States. The position of the United Automobile Workers has been that the producers can afford to pay wage parity and still eliminate the differential. We do not feel that the available data are sufficient to take a firm position one way or the other on this point. For our purposes here, we would simply note that the comparative

---

[13]Note that a big jump in the differential occurred in 1968, the initial year in a three-year contract which will gradually bring about wage parity in the U.S. and Canadian plants of the main vehicle-producers.

prices of vehicles in Canada and the United States are irrelevant to the decision as to where additional production facilities will be located once the conditions for duty-free trade contained in the Agreement and the letters of undertaking have been met. Comparative price levels affect the distribution of costs and benefits arising from the Agreement but not the distribution of production; comparative wage rates affect both.

C. Comparative Vehicle Prices

Table 25 shows the pattern of factory list prices in Canada and the United States during 1964 through 1969. Differences due to sales taxes and variations in equipment have been eliminated in this series. If prices of other vehicles have performed similarly, we can see that the differential between Canada and the United States has narrowed considerably, but a noticeable margin remains.[14]

There are three reasons that might be cited in justification for higher vehicle prices in Canada following the Agreement:

1)   The integration of the two sectors of the industry resulted in a decline in the value of certain Canadian assets of the vehicle-producers that were unsuited for production in an integrated North American market. No figures are publicly available on the amount of this capital loss, and we cannot even be certain that it was greater than the duties that had formerly been paid but that were no longer required as a result of the Agreement. In any event, this factor would not be the basis for continuing price differentials once the capital loss had been recovered. We would also note that while the vehicle-producers had an effective means for making up any loss through the prices they charged in Canada, the independent parts-manufacturers in both countries also faced capital losses which were much more difficult to recoup.

2)   The cost of distribution and sales in Canada may be higher than in the United States. This could be the result, for example, of differences in the costs of servicing warranties and of an inability to spread specific Canadian administrative costs, such as legal and customs documentation expenses, over as large a sales volume. Again, no precise estimates of the size of any cost differences of this nature are available.

3)   Finally, and most important for our analysis, restrictions on free trade, either those contained in the Agreement and the letters of undertaking or any further conditions in the future designed to maintain a particular share of production in Canada, may lead to excess production

---

[14]We have been informed by one of the manufacturers that if the prices of commercial vehicles were compared in a similar manner, the differential would be less than for cars.

costs in North America. The differential between Canadian and U.S. vehicle prices will determine which country pays what proportion of the burden of any such cost excess.

TABLE 25

COMPARATIVE PASSENGER-CAR PRICES, 1964-69[a]
(U.S. dollars)

| | Price in U.S. | Price in Canada[b] | Canadian Price Differential over U.S. Price | |
			Amount	Percent
Valiant				
1964	2,137	2,342	205	9.6
1965	2,147	2,353	206	9.6
1966	2,197	2,356	159	7.2
1967	2,242	2,394	152	6.8
1968	2,337	2,470	133	5.7
1969	2,384	2,483	99	4.2
Ford Custom				
1964	2,529	2,762	233	9.2
1965	2,539	2,773	234	9.2
1966	2,597	2,769	172	6.6
1967	2,639	2,806	167	6.3
1968	2,734	2,894	160	5.9
1969	2,868	3,027	159	5.6
Buick Riviera				
1964	3,995	5,209	1,214	30.4
1965	4,026	5,256	1,230	30.6
1966	4,127	5,145	1,018	24.7
1967	4,169	5,184	1,015	24.3
1968	4,283	4,655	372	8.7
1969	4,510	4,960	450	10.0

[a]Factory list prices of comparably equipped models.
[b]Expressed in U.S. dollars at the exchange rate of U.S. $0.925 = Can. $1.

Sources: *Second Annual Report of the President to the Congress on the Operation of the Automotive Products Trade Act of 1965* (Washington: U.S. Government Printing Office, 1968), pp. 40-42. Also, *Third Annual Report...,* 1969, pp. 16-17. The identity of these models was revealed in *Canadian Automobile Agreement,* Hearing before the Committee on Finance, United States Senate, 90th Congress, 2nd Session, July 19, 1968, p. 15.

These reasons explain why price differentials might exist because of cost differentials. The information that is publicly available is totally inadequate to be able to assert that existing price differentials can, in fact, be completely attributed to cost factors. While we conclude that the extent of overfulfillment of Canadian value-added requirements by the producers (Table 21) proves that production costs on a portion of this output were no greater than in the United States, this does not mean that total costs of all Canadian output were low enough to warrant the elimination of the price spread.

D. Economic Impact of Changes in Production Shares

It will be recalled from the discussion in Chapter 5 that we shared the view of proponents of the Agreement that it was not a "zero-sum game" in which one country's gains had to come at the expense of equal losses by the other. The rapid progress towards specialization, detailed in Chapter 6, confirms the contention that very considerable over-all efficiency gains were possible through restructuring the Canadian sector of the industry to serve an integrated North American market. These efficiency gains brought about an increase in the total economic welfare of North America; and provided that Canada's gain did not exhaust the amount of the increase, there were possibilities for gains in the United States as well. There would still be the question of how gains and losses were distributed among various interest groups in both countries — employees, independent parts-producers, etc. — but so long as over-all gains were possible, there need not have been any net losers if appropriate means of compensation were devised.

Unfortunately, this is not all that was involved. Even though the United States did not have to suffer economic losses matching any gains made in Canada, net U.S. losses could be involved in the wake of changes in shares of North American automotive production that have resulted from the Agreement. The purpose of the analysis in this chapter has been to bring us to the point where we can discuss with more precision the nature and probable extent of these losses.

Let us begin with the fact that the U.S. balance on automotive trade with Canada declined by U.S.$357 million between 1964 and 1968 (Table 21) and by a substantial additional amount during 1969 (Table 23). What has been the real economic cost of this development to the United States?

Regardless of why this decline in sales to Canada occurred, the fact that there was a decline means that factors of production in the United States — labour, capital, raw materials — that would otherwise have been employed in producing these automotive products for sale in Canada must find alternative occupations. This leads to the following possibilities for economic losses:

1) If factors previously engaged in automotive production must find permanent employment in other industries, there will be costs of retraining and relocating workers and of scrapping specialized equipment at a capital loss. Our discussion at the beginning of this chapter suggests that losses from this source have been very small in the United States because of continued long-term growth in aggregate North American demand for automotive products.

2)   If factors employed in the automotive industry receive wages and rents that are above the average in the economy as a whole because of various market imperfections, the sales decline transfers a portion of the excess to Canada. It is very difficult to measure exactly how much, if any, loss this may involve. Even if we could calculate an amount, we would be unable to find a sound economic justification for arguing that the proceeds on sales to Canada arising from market imperfections should accrue to the United States. Nevertheless, since the bulk of the Canadian automotive industry consists of subsidiaries of American parents, excessive rents paid to equity capital would ultimately resort back to the United States except for that portion taxed to Canada. This factor may represent a significant offset to any losses to the United States arising from the Agreement, and we will return to the point in a moment.

3)   The decline in sales to Canada tends to reduce the foreign-exchange earnings of the United States. It is here that the analysis becomes further complicated, so we will consider this question in some detail.

Up to this point we have concentrated upon the effects of the Agreement in terms of the balance on automotive trade between Canada and the United States. This measure, provided it is accurately defined (see Section C of Chapter 7 and Appendix E), is the best indicator of changes in production shares in the automotive industry alone, but it gives a wholly mistaken impression of the size of losses to the United States. While it is true that a decline in net sales to Canada has resulted in a drop in potential employment opportunities in the American automotive industry, the impact of the Agreement in terms of the over-all economic interests of the United States should be measured on the basis of total balance of payments effects. These contain at least three offsetting effects:

1)   There would be an increase of U.S. exports of non-automotive (i.e., non-automotive as defined by the Agreement) products to Canada that would not otherwise have occurred.

2)   Some of the U.S. resources released by the decline in automotive sales to Canada are available to produce goods that are either exported to third countries or substituted for U.S. imports.[15]

---

[15]A very good case can be made for arguing that these first two offsets have been particularly large thus far during the life of the Agreement. During most of this period, full employment and inflationary demand conditions prevailed in the United States (and Canada as well). Therefore, if the United States had supplied the same proportion of the Canadian automotive market as prior to the Agreement, it would have added to an already excessive demand on its resources, putting further pressure on prices and the balance of trade in non-automotive products. The long-range impact of the Agreement, however, should not be judged on the basis of short-term economic conditions.

3) Earnings, service fees, etc., would be remitted from Canada by subsidiaries of American parents. This class of payments from Canadian subsidiaries increases the foreign-exchange earnings of the United States and acts as an offset in just the same way as the other two factors listed above. To the extent that the growth in these payments is the result of increased investment outflows from the United States, some adjustment may be desirable to take account of differences in the timing of inflows and outflows; but we think this is a rather minor consideration in the case of the Agreement.[16] There is, however, a very important distinction that must be made in the treatment of these payments.

Once the total impact of the Agreement on the size of foreign-exchange earnings of the United States has been calculated, inclusive of the offsets listed, we have a measure of gross losses to the United States. As we shall see shortly, the net loss from this source will most likely be a very small fraction of the gross loss. Now, if the payments from Canadian subsidiaries represent returns to U.S.-owned assets that exceed amounts that could be earned if these assets were employed in the United States, the net economic welfare of the United States increases by the full amount of the difference. And the very same conclusion holds for any increase in the earnings potential of U.S.-owned assets abroad, even though, as in the case of unremitted earnings of foreign subsidiaries, no balance of payments entry is made in the official U.S. statistics. The significance of this distinction will emerge as we continue.

This list indicates the kind of information that would be required to calculate the balance of payments impact of the Agreement. If either government has made such a calculation, it has not released it, nor has it stressed the necessity for attempting to carry out the exercise. This is indeed unfortunate, since by concentrating on the balance of automotive trade alone (especially when the statistics reported in the two countries are full of weaknesses — see Appendix E), a misleading picture of the Agreement is presented, and one which encourages an overly pessimistic appraisal on the U.S. side.

Given the scope of the task and the unavailability of certain basic data, no attempt to perform this necessary calculation will be made here. However, on the basis of the limited data that are available and assumptions regarding likely magnitudes where they are not, it is fairly certain that a permanent loss of automotive sales to Canada in the amounts experienced thus far would constitute a noticeable negative impact on the U.S. balance of payments position, but one that is considerably less than might appear from automotive trade statistics alone.

---

[16]Although evidence is very scarce, the manufacturers claim that the restructuring required by the Agreement has been financed almost exclusively in Canada. In any event, adjustments for timing of inflows and outflows presuppose near-term balance of payments difficulties in the United States.

What, then, is the economic cost of a negative development in terms of the balance of payments position of the United States? We are not certain about the answer because we cannot predict what a net reduction in foreign-exchange receipts by the United States will require by way of adjustment. There is no doubt that if the reduction were too great, there could be a serious impact on the international position of the dollar. The repercussions of a significant permanent decline in the proportion of the Canadian automotive market supplied from the United States probably fall far short of this amount unless one considers that the dollar is already weak and any incremental negative factor is too great to be withstood. We do not think the dollar is in any serious danger of declining in value relative to other currencies, but there are valid differences of opinion on its strength.

About all we can say is that in our judgment the most likely consequence will be that the international financial position of the United States will improve by a somewhat smaller amount than otherwise. That is, while the growth of all U.S. claims on foreigners will continue to outpace the growth of all foreign claims on the United States, the amount of net improvement will be diminished by some fraction of the decline in U.S. automotive sales to Canada.

If this turns out to be the case, the loss to the United States will be the return that could have been earned on a larger international "net worth" position. Even then, it must be remembered that the lower rate of growth in net assets held abroad stems from a transfer of U.S. resources from occupations giving rise to foreign-exchange earnings. If these resources are employed productively at home, they too will earn a return that can be set against the loss in the international sector.

There is one final and highly important topic to be considered. Thus far we have assumed a change in shares of North American automotive production as a result of the Agreement and have made no distinction regarding the cause of the change. There are two alternatives:

1) If protection is the cause, costs in Canada will be excessive in relation to U.S. costs for the same output. If prices in Canada fully reflect this cost difference, there will be no additional loss to the United States beyond that described above. However, to the extent that Canadian demand for North American-produced vehicles is responsive to changes in price, these excess costs will retard growth in Canadian consumption, a portion of which might be supplied from the United States.[17]

---

[17]This factor will be relevant to the United States only if Canada does not insist upon producing as much as it consumes.

2)   If market forces are the cause, there is a potential gain to be set against the loss described above. Unless prices in Canada decline by the full amount of the cost savings arising from these market forces, earnings of American subsidiaries will rise; and just possibly, vehicle prices in the United States will be lower than otherwise. The full amount of these gains to the United States should be compared with the net losses arising from the balance of payments impact to arrive at the over-all economic cost or benefit of the Agreement to the United States.

This chapter has raised a number of complex technical issues in an effort to give a sense of perspective to the possible economic cost to the United States of participation in a trade pact that has resulted in a significant net decline in its automotive sales to Canada. We regret that we have been unable to calculate the amount of the cost, if any, but the governments involved, who have much of the basic information required, have not made this calculation either. It is essential that this exercise be performed because certain interest groups in the United States may argue that the Agreement has been detrimental to them, even though the real cause for any distress is to be found in other developments. By concentrating on the size of the sales decline alone, a very inaccurate view of over-all economic gains or losses to the United States is given, and this would provide a poor framework for assessing the need for policy changes.

In the next chapter, which concludes this study, we will analyze the issues that have been raised by the Agreement within the context of possible policy options for the future.

10

Alternatives for the Future

In June, 1969, the U.S. Department of State requested that the two governments initiate a series of joint meetings to consider the results of the Agreement to date and the alternative courses for future action. These meetings began in Washington in November, 1969, and are continuing as this is written. The only substantive result to emerge thus far has been an agreement to establish a subcommittee to investigate the problems of reconciling production and trade statistics in the two countries.

The question that is really at issue in these meetings is not statistics — it is the fact that both governments are dissatisfied with the Agreement as it now stands, but for very different reasons. Our discussion in the preceding chapter provides the basis for analyzing the issues in terms of future policy options; but before turning to this topic, there are certain questions concerning statistics that require clarification.

Our investigation of the subject leads us to conclude that there are very few serious gaps in the data at the disposal of the two governments for purposes of determining the effects of the Agreement; the primary problems are those of reporting and analysis. As we indicate in Appendix E (Part IV), none of the methods that have been used for reporting changes in the balance of automotive trade are adequate for appraising the impact of the Agreement. But even this is of relatively minor consequence when it is recognized that changes in this balance alone produce a grossly exaggerated impression of gains and losses in terms of the over-all economic interests of the two countries (see Section D, Chapter 9).

With respect to comparisons of production efficiency in the two sectors of the industry, Canada insists that its efficiency is still somewhat

123

below that in the United States because transitional adjustments are incomplete; but the statistics necessary to prove this assertion are unreported, and the assumptions upon which it is based remain unexplained. In any event, we shall demonstrate in this chapter that it is not comparative production efficiency alone that will determine the long-term effects of the Agreement, but comparative efficiency in relation to comparative wage rates.

The basic position adopted by the United States during the current series of intergovernmental meetings stems from the fact that Canadian automotive production has expanded by substantially more than would have been necessary simply to meet the conditions in the Agreement and the letters of undertaking. In Section D, Chapter 7, it was shown that as of 1968 all conditions had been exceeded by a wide margin. Most important, the overfulfillment in terms of total Canadian value added amounted to U.S.$396 million in 1968 (Table 21); when the complete results are in for 1969, the figure will be much greater.[1]

The United States contends that the objectives of the Agreement (see Article I, Appendix A, and Section A, Chapter 9) are to achieve unrestricted free trade in the North American automotive industry. Furthermore, it is argued, the conditions imposed upon the producers by the Canadian government were meant to be *transitional* safeguards only; and given the increase in Canadian production that has taken place in excess of that needed to meet these conditions, it is time to begin removing them.[2]

Canada contends that the overriding objective of the Agreement is to enable "the industries of both countries to participate on a fair and equitable basis in the expanding total market of the two countries" [Article I(b)]. Canada defines "fair and equitable" in this context to mean equality or near equality between its production and consumption of automotive products. Canada would probably admit that in the recent past this objective has been met, but it would be dissatisfied with a long-term performance that did no more than satisfy the conditions in the Agreement and the letters of undertaking as they now stand (Section B, Chapter 8).

---

[1]We did not wish to delay this study until all the results for the full year 1969 were available, and thus decided to forego attempts at a precise estimate based on part-year data. But on the basis of trade statistics for the first nine months of 1969 (Table 23) and other part-year information that was available, it is anticipated that overfulfillment of constraints as they existed in 1969 will reach some U.S.$700 million for the full year. Events in the last several months of the year might alter this by as much as U.S.$100 million up or down. To give some perspective to this figure, *total* value added in Canadian automotive industries during 1963 was U.S.$709 million (see Table 4, Chapter 2).

[2]"In view of these industry and trade developments, it would seem timely to move toward elimination of the transitional restrictions on Canadian imports of motor vehicles and parts from the United States." *Third Annual Report . . ., op. cit.,* p. 2.

We have found no evidence that Canada regards the need for aggregate production guarantees as being a transitional phenomenon.

Quite clearly, the meetings now under way between the two governments must address basic issues that should have been resolved at the time the Agreement was negotiated. We cannot predict what the outcome will be, but the framework that was provided in the preceding chapter enables us to assess the probable economic consequences of the various policy options.

There is one very important last point by way of introduction. Canada is now in an awkward position regarding the future of the Agreement. It is Canada that has increased its share of production very substantially, and it is Canada that has applied the restraints on North American free trade in automotive products. Therefore, the United States has very little to lose in the short run by arguing for removal of the Canadian restrictions.

But suppose that Canada takes a gamble involving some risks — although we think they are relatively small — and removes all restrictions on the producers. Can Canada also count on at least a chance of a further gain in the form of an even larger share of North American automotive production without restrictions, explicit or implicit, on the U.S. side? And would the United States be so anxious for unrestricted free trade if the Canadian affiliate of the UAW had not been successful in obtaining wage "parity" with the employees in the United States?

These questions may not be theoretical by any means. It could well turn out that when all the advantages and the disadvantages of locating additional facilities in Canada are weighed, the differential between real and nominal wage parity might cause the vehicle-producers to expand more rapidly there than in the United States. And in the case of independent parts-producers who do not even have to pay nominal parity as yet, the advantages of expansion in Canada might be even greater. It is our view that questions of this sort were not asked or answered properly at the time the Agreement was negotiated, but they must be now that critical decisions concerning the future of the Agreement are being formulated. We turn, therefore, to a discussion of possible options for modifying and/or extending the Agreement.

A. Possible Changes in the Provisions of the Formal Agreement[3]

1. In-Vehicle Canadian Content

The formal Agreement between the two governments contains a provision requiring Canadian producers to maintain the same total dollar

---

[3]The reader is referred to Section A.2, Chapter 4, and Annex A in Appendix A for a more complete description of the provisions discussed in this section.

amount of Canadian content (value added) in Canadian-produced vehicles as in the 1964 model year (August 1, 1963, to July 31, 1964). This condition had only one purpose originally: to provide protection for Canadian parts-producers during the period of transitional adjustment to the Agreement. As total vehicle production in Canada has grown, the in-vehicle content required per unit has fallen substantially (Table 12, Chapter 6), and in most cases this condition can be fulfilled with the value added achieved in simple assembly operations supplemented by parts produced efficiently in Canada for the entire North American market.

This provision no longer serves its original purpose effectively, but acts instead as either a nuisance factor or a barrier to maximum efficiency in Canadian operations, particularly those of the smaller firms (American Motors and International Harvester) and Chrysler's truck division. The removal of the provision would increase the efficiency of Canadian and North American automotive production, but probably at the cost to Canada of some portion of its share of total output. This conclusion follows from the fact that, with an ample excess in the total amount of Canadian value added (in-vehicle and other) over the commitments in the letters of undertaking (Table 21), some manufacturers would shift to the United States any high-cost production currently needed to fill out the in-vehicle content requirement. As vehicle production in Canada expands, however, this shift will take place anyway, so all that Canada really gains from this condition is a little more time.

2. Production-to-Sales Ratios for Vehicles

The second condition that the Agreement places upon Canadian producers is that the ratio of their vehicle production to their sales in Canada must be as great as that achieved during the 1964 model year or 75 percent, whichever is higher. This condition, like the in-vehicle content provision, must be satisfied for each class of vehicle (cars, trucks, buses) produced by the manufacturer. Because of the very sharp increase in Canadian assembly activity following the Agreement, the minimum ratio has been exceeded by a wide margin in the aggregate, but the Canadian truck production of Chrysler and International Harvester remains at nearly the level of their sales in Canada (see Table 10, Chapter 6).

Changes in this condition might take two forms. First, the ratio might be made to apply to total vehicle production for each manufacturer, so that it would be possible for, say, Chrysler to phase out truck assembly in Canada if that were desirable, substituting instead a greater amount of assembly in cars if this were necessary to fill out the aggregate production-to-sales requirement. This change would increase the efficiency of Canadian and North American automotive production; but as with changes in the in-vehicle content provision, this modification would probably cost Canada a portion of its share of output. Given the present overfulfillment of the total Canadian value-added commitments in the letters of undertaking plus an excess in assembly over that required to meet the production-to-sales ratios, the ability to cut down on the production of a high-cost class of vehicles would not require the manufacturer to add a compensating amount of value added in other areas.

The second possibility for modifying the production-to-sales provision would be to reduce the required ratio or to eliminate it entirely. There are a number of problems which complicate the analysis of such suggestions.

1) Given the differences in the collective bargaining strength of workers employed by independent parts-producers and the vehicle-manufacturers, it is possible for Canada to have a real advantage (in Canada only) in assembly but an apparent advantage in parts production. In other words, the amount of real resources required to produce a unit of output in assembly may be lower than in parts, but money costs, inclusive of wage differentials, might indicate the reverse. In this case the protection of assembly operations contained in the production-to-sales ratio requirements (with no distinction by vehicle class) may encourage efficient automotive production in Canada.

2) The situation with respect to North American efficiency in automotive production might be just the opposite, with Canada having a relative advantage in parts and the United States having a relative advantage in assembly. Given the vehicle production-to-sales condition, however, a shift in Canadian resources from assembly to parts production would be impossible.

3) As if the question were not complicated enough already, the production-to-sales requirement is the most effective device Canada has in the Agreement for assuring a greater share of production than would be based solely on production costs or commitments in the present letters of undertaking. As we have discussed in Section A.3 of Chapter 8, assembly plants have to be built and operated at a fairly large scale relative to the size of the Canadian market in order to reach peak efficiency. Therefore, unless the manufacturers were willing and able to alter their production and purchases of parts in Canada with considerable flexibility, the production-to-sales ratio would usually guarantee that Canadian automotive output would be well above the minimum required to meet other commitments.

3. Duty-Free Treatment in Canada for Manufacturers Only

Table 25 in the preceding chapter showed that the differential in the factory list price of comparable vehicles sold in Canada and the United States has narrowed considerably following the Agreement, but a noticeable margin remains. One possibility for eliminating this differential would be to extend the opportunity for duty-free vehicle imports to all Canadians.[4] This proposal raises a number of rather complex questions, not the least of which are procedural. For instance, differences in sales taxes in the two countries would create certain difficulties in the case of direct importation. These problems could be worked out through some method of documentation at the border, but some increase in administrative costs might be involved. A much more important procedural issue relates to the fact that Canada would probably have to obtain a GATT waiver — as the United States has had to do — if this modification were put through, since it is most unlikely that free entry would apply to automotive imports from third countries (see Section E, Chapter 5).

But beyond the procedural problems lies the very difficult — and unasked — question of whether prices in Canada *should* be the same as those in the United States, once an adjustment has been made for transport, tax, and exchange differences. We cannot answer this question categorically, but the following points have a bearing on the issue:

1) The location of automotive production in North America will be determined by comparative production costs and production guarantees, not by relative prices. If Canada were to achieve price parity through allowing all Canadians to import vehicles duty-free, there would be almost no way to exert effective conditions on the value of production by the Canadian manufacturers.

2) Because of the fact that the Agreement was of primary direct benefit to production and employment in the Toronto-Windsor region, the main benefit to the rest of Canada is the extent to which vehicle prices there fall relative to those in the United States.

3) If we assume that vehicle demand is at all responsive to price changes, a lowering of the relative price differential will make North American vehicles more attractive in Canada, thereby increasing total production and employment opportunities in both countries and reducing reliance upon third-country imports.[5]

---

[4]Since prices have remained higher in Canada than in the United States, the right of any American to import a vehicle duty-free from Canada has been one in theory rather than practice.

[5]Table 2 and Chart 1 in Chapter 1 indicate that the differential between Canadian and U.S. purchases of third-country vehicles has narrowed considerably since 1962. We hesitate to attribute this exclusively to the price differential between Canada and the United States, but lower relative prices in Canada since the Agreement have undoubtedly been one factor.

4) Price discrimination can be said to exist when costs are the same and prices differ *or* when prices are the same and costs differ. Because the Canadian vehicle-manufacturers are subsidiaries of American firms, Canada has a special interest in avoiding the first type of discrimination, while the United States has a special interest in avoiding the second type. This brings us to the heart of a problem raised in the preceding chapter, namely, whether the Agreement has led to an over-all economic loss to the United States. This point merits elaboration.

The main issue concerning the price differential on vehicles is the determination of how efficiency gains arising from the Agreement are to be distributed.[6] Part of these gains have been channeled to Canadian automotive workers in the form of higher wages. The remainder have been divided between lower relative prices to the Canadian consumer and higher profits to the manufacturers (although we cannot estimate the relative proportion going to each group on the basis of available statistics). The greater the extent of the price differential that is not explained by cost differences, the greater the returns to the United States (since the main producers in Canada are owned primarily by Americans) from the Agreement.

We concluded in the preceding chapter that no accurate assessment of the Agreement's impact on over-all U.S. economic interests can be made until the effects on profits of American firms with subsidiaries in Canada have been determined. The vehicle price differential may provide a means, albeit an inefficient one, for the United States to more than recoup the economic losses involved in the decline in vehicle sales to Canada.[7]

B. Changes in the Letters of Undertaking[8]

Removal of the in-vehicle content requirement and the production-to-sales ratios in the formal Agreement could increase the efficiency of North American automotive production. Canada is not really concerned

---

[6]Efficiency gains were not the only factor, since the manufacturers were able to recoup any of the duties on automotive imports prior to the Agreement (see Section D, Chapter 5).
[7]This conclusion leaves a number of significant questions unresolved. Among the more important is that even though the vehicle-producers and the United States as a whole may have benefited from the Agreement, other interest groups may have lost. This does not appear to have been a major problem in this particular case because buoyant vehicle demand in the United States prevented permanent lay-offs and absolute sales declines in the industry (see Chapter 9). But this does not negate the fact that trade agreements can have harmful effects on certain groups, and it is a challenge to policy-makers to prevent unequal distribution of gains and losses through appropriate assistance programs — funded, preferably, by those who benefit from the agreement.
[8]The letters, a sample of which appears in Appendix B, are discussed in detail in Section B, Chapter 4.

with these conditions as such: it wants further commitments of the kind contained in the original letters of undertaking. These commitments constrain the producers to achieve a specific level of aggregate value added in Canadian automotive production, but there are no restrictions as to how this value added is to be obtained.

As we have stated before, it is this issue of additional production guarantees that is at the centre of debate between the two countries. On the one hand, the whole episode of the original undertakings was handled very poorly from the point of view of U.S. politics, since they were negotiated in secret and excluded from the formal Agreement itself. This fact, plus the marked decline in net U.S. automotive sales to Canada that has taken place, means that any additions to the original commitments, even through informal understandings, would lead to strong pressures in the U.S. Congress to discontinue the Agreement. And if such a move were made during a cyclical sales slump in the industry, such as is taking place as this is written, these pressures would stand a fair chance of succeeding.

On the other hand, if Canadian automotive production performs too poorly in the years ahead, Canada also has the right to abrogate the Agreement. Regardless of which country initiated the move, abrogation would cause a return to the original situation in the industry, which led to other attempted remedies that threatened to cause serious strains in Canadian-American economic relations.

In the remainder of this chapter we will consider the economic case for resolving the issues raised by the Agreement through extension of North American free trade to other commodities. But first, we recognize that a verdict to expand North American free trade will rest on much more than economic effects — let alone theory. Therefore, we offer the following comments concerning the issue of production guarantees based on the discussion in this and preceding chapters:

1) If a production guarantee is granted to Canada at a level that raises the cost of North American automotive production above the minimum attainable amount, there is a vehicle price differential that would enable Canada, through the profits of American subsidiaries, to bear the entire burden of the excess. In other words, if Canada is dead set upon achieving a specific relationship between automotive production and sales there and is willing to pay the price for any excess costs involved, the United States would suffer no additional economic loss in assisting Canada to reduce excess costs by producing that output for the entire North American market. The real cost in this case is the political ill will that arises from Canada's decision to press for this production-sales objective.

2) But suppose Canada consents to unrestricted North American free trade in automotive products and removes the present conditions on the producers after some specified time interval. There is, in our opinion, little chance that the U.S. automotive trade balance with Canada will be restored to anywhere near the surplus that was observed prior to the Agreement. On the contrary, Canada may have a surplus in the future if market forces are allowed to determine location decisions.[9] The biggest uncertainty is the behaviour of comparative wage rates, and we believe that if wages in Canada were to conform to average productivity in the Canadian economy as a whole rather than to wage levels in the United States, there would be no doubt about a Canadian automotive trade surplus. Even nominal rather than real wage parity (see Section B, Chapter 9) could be enough to shift the balance in Canada's favour, and the fundamental weakness in the original predictions of the Agreement's effects (Section A, Chapter 4) was that no real attempt was made to determine the answer to this question. Given the excessive concern on both sides concerning automotive trade-balance impacts, a possible *quid pro quo* political compromise might be to set a maximum as well as a minimum limit on the share of North American automotive production in Canada. This would definitely be an inefficient solution in terms of the over-all economic interests of both countries. But the solution would be superior to the consequences of a return to the pre-Agreement situation which abrogation on either side might bring, and this may be the alternative with which policy-makers are some day faced.

3) Restrictions on free trade in automotive products in any form will require difficult decisions regarding the vehicle price differential in the two countries. Only in the event of unrestricted free trade could it be said with certainty that vehicle prices, corrected for tax and exchange differences, should be the same in both countries. So long as restrictions remain, the question will be to judge the appropriateness of any differential, and the answer to this question is as important to the economic interests of the United States (because of profit effects) as it is to those of Canada.

C. Expanding the Commodity Coverage of the Agreement

Reports of the current bilateral negotiations indicate that one possibility under consideration is the extension of the Agreement to include specialty vehicles, replacement parts, and possibly tires. There are a number of reasons why expansion along these lines might be considered useful by some parties.

---

[9]There would still be the issue of possible U.S. government interference in the locational decisions of the parent vehicle-producers, which is a major concern in Canada. We make no comment on this issue because it is essentially a political rather than an economic matter, and there is some doubt that it can ever be completely resolved to the satisfaction of both countries.

1) Replacement parts are usually difficult to distinguish from original parts, thereby creating problems in customs administration. In addition, even those products that are shipped by the vehicle-producers to service their new-car warranties are classified as replacement parts, paying full duty. Given the predominance of U.S. parts, this factor tends to raise the cost of vehicles sold in Canada somewhat, although we cannot estimate the amount.

2) Certain stages in the construction of some specialty vehicles (fire engines, vehicles modified for integration with cranes, etc.), which are excluded from the Agreement, may be subject to economies of scale that could be more fully realized through free trade.

3) Since tires mounted on new vehicles can be entered into either country duty-free and since Canada has greatly expanded its net exports of completed vehicles (see Table 19, Chapter 7), U.S.-made tires may have lost part of their share in the North American market.

While the interests of economic efficiency could be served by extending the Agreement to include as many products as possible, the basic groundwork to determine the probable locational effects of these changes has not been done. One gets the strong impression that proposals for expanding the scope of the Agreement are motivated by a desire to make certain effects of the present Agreement more palatable or to use them as bargaining devices for achieving other modifications. If this is indeed true, the danger is that the issues that have proven controversial in the past will be extended into other sectors.

The question of expanding the scope of the present Agreement is really a variant of the general question of whether further attempts at sectoral free trade in North America are desirable. We turn to this issue in conclusion.

D. The Need for a Long-Term Commitment

Let us digress for a moment and ask why it is that Canada has been so concerned about closing the gap between its production and consumption of automotive products. There are some in Canada who still accept the simple and basically unsound proposition that a viable automotive industry is a sign of economic maturity. In other countries, including the United States, the same appeal has been made for steel, chemicals, oil-refining, and a host of other sectors. This argument contradicts the basic rationale for international trade, which is to achieve mutual gains through specialization in those activities in which countries have a comparative advantage.

Another, more sophisticated argument is that, for reasons of domestic employment or balance of payments considerations, a nation cannot allow foreign producers to gain too great a share of a home market as vital as automotive products. Again, the United States can be included in a long list of nations that have sought to limit foreign penetration in textiles, computers, aircraft, and numerous other products on similar grounds. Regardless of how refined the arguments become, the protection of domestic activity in any industry brings with it a lower level of total economic welfare than would otherwise be possible.

As a result of the Automotive Agreement, however, Canada now has an interesting and valid reason for wanting to maximize the amount of automotive output it produces. Because free trade, even though conditioned by various constraints, has sharply reduced the inefficiencies in Canadian automotive production, the average productivity of Canadian resources would undoubtedly rise with greater concentration of these resources in the automotive sector. In other words, if the resources cannot be utilized at least as productively elsewhere, why not try to achieve the greatest possible share of the North American automotive market?

The United States, of course, is unlikely to see things this way. It too may feel that the resources devoted to its automotive industry are more — or at least no less — productive than the over-all average achieved in the economy as a whole. Thus an economic conflict of interest develops, and it is our contention that this same conflict would arise in any further piecemeal attempt at sectoral free trade in North America.

In the sector chosen for free trade there will be a tendency for Canadian employment to decline or the U.S. share of North American output in the industry to fall, and there is a chance that both developments will occur simultaneously. This conclusion follows from the fact that simply because efficiency gains are the object of free trade, the number of workers required to produce a given volume of output will decline. Since these efficiency gains can be expected to be greater in relation to Canadian productivity prior to free trade, Canada would have to expand its share of North American output to avoid a decline in employment.

Offsetting the tendencies listed above will be the increase in North American consumption made possible by the gains in economic efficiency. But the increase in consumption will tend to be spread among all products, and the more selective is the list of industries involved in free trade, the lower the potential for expanding total North American production and employment in those chosen industries.

The economic cost to the United States of a decline in its share of North American production resulting from one sectoral free trade pact, the Automotive Agreement, could have been much more serious if it were not for the fact that Americans own most of the Canadian industry and benefit directly from rising profits there or if it had not turned out that North American automotive purchases expanded rapidly during most of the period. These factors might not be present in other sectors.

Therefore, any further sectoral trade agreements between Canada and the United States will require, at a minimum, the selection of a group of industries including those for which each country must be prepared to experience some loss of employment at worst and some decline in its share of North American output at best.

It would be possible, through a process of careful selection, to put together a group of industries for which free trade would be mutually beneficial to the over-all economic interests of both Canada and the United States. If such a course were adopted, the background of the Automotive Agreement suggests that Canada should be aware that U.S. acceptance will depend not only on economic effects but also on such factors as procedures with the Congress and, most important, an initiative that does not arise out of unilateral Canadian actions.[10]

But while the possibility of moving towards free trade by groups of sectors may be feasible and even desirable from an economic point of view, a long-term commitment to North American free trade in all manufactured products might be preferable, particularly in terms of Canada's own over-all economic interests.

The basic economic objection to limited free trade is that it would create serious distortions and strains on those Canadian sectors that are excluded, and the degree to which this occurs will increase as the list of free-trade industries broadens. Specifically, there will be, as in the automotive industry following the Agreement, strong pressures in the chosen industries to close the gap in U.S. and Canadian wage rates as free trade tends to equalize the productivity in the two countries. Those industries unable to achieve the productivity gains produced by free trade will also experience these wage pressures, with the probable result that their prices will rise relative to those of free-traded goods, causing declining sales opportunities and increased import penetration.

In this section we have moved a long way from our original study of the workings of the 1965 Automotive Agreement. There are numerous pros and cons, both economic and political, on the issue of general free trade between Canada and the United States on both sides of the border. The economic feasibility for Canada of broad free trade with the United States has been established with considerable precision and clarity else-

---

[10]Sperry Lea, "Free Trade by Sectors," *Looking Ahead* (Washington: National Planning Association, September, 1966), p. 1.

where.[11] No attempt to elaborate on this topic will be made here because to do so would take us too far afield from our primary purposes. We would say in conclusion, however, that the operation of the Agreement has shown for one sector how great the benefits can be from gearing Canadian production to the entire North American market rather than to a small domestic market isolated by tariff barriers at home and abroad. But if further moves in this direction are judged desirable, a basis must be found for allocating the benefits in a manner which will be satisfactory to both countries.

---

[11]Ronald J. Wonnacott and Paul Wonnacott, *Free Trade Beween the United States and Canada, op. cit.*

Part IV:
APPENDICES

Appendix A

Agreement Concerning Automotive Products
Between the Government of the United States of America
and the Government of Canada

The Government of the United States of America and the Government of Canada,

Determined to strengthen the economic relations between their two countries;

Recognizing that this can best be achieved through the stimulation of economic growth and through the expansion of markets available to producers in both countries within the framework of the established policy of both countries of promoting multilateral trade;

Recognizing that an expansion of trade can best be achieved through the reduction or elimination of tariff and all other barriers to trade operating to impede or distort the full and efficient development of each country's trade and industrial potential;

Recognizing the important place that the automotive industry occupies in the industrial economy of the two countries and the interests of industry, labor and consumers in sustaining high levels of efficient production and continued growth in the automotive industry;

Agree as follows:

Article I

The Governments of the United States and Canada, pursuant to the above principles, shall seek the early achievement of the following objectives:

(a) The creation of a broader market for automotive products within which the full benefits of specialization and large-scale production can be achieved;

(b) The liberalization of United States and Canadian automotive trade in respect of tariff barriers and other factors tending

139

to impede it, with a view to enabling the industries of both countries to participate on a fair and equitable basis in the expanding total market of the two countries;

(c) The development of conditions in which market forces may operate effectively to attain the most economic pattern of investment, production and trade.

It shall be the policy of each Government to avoid actions which would frustrate the achievement of these objectives.

Article II

(a) The Government of Canada, not later than the entry into force of the legislation contemplated in paragraph (b) of this Article, shall accord duty-free treatment to imports of the products of the United States described in Annex A.

(b) The Government of the United States, during the session of the United States Congress commencing on January 4, 1965, shall seek enactment of legislation authorizing duty-free treatment of imports of the products of Canada described in Annex B. In seeking such legislation, the Government of the United States shall also seek authority permitting the implementation of such duty-free treatment retroactively to the earliest date administratively possible following the date upon which the Government of Canada has accorded duty-free treatment. Promptly after the entry into force of such legislation, the Government of the United States shall accord duty-free treatment to the products of Canada described in Annex B.

Article III

The commitments made by the two Governments in this Agreement shall not preclude action by either Government consistent with its obligations under Part II of the General Agreement on Tariffs and Trade.

Article IV

(a) At any time, at the request of either Government, the two Governments shall consult with respect to any matter relating to this Agreement.

(b) Without limiting the foregoing, the two Governments shall, at the request of either Government, consult with respect to any problems which may arise concerning automotive producers in the United States which do not at present have facilities in Canada for the manufacture of motor vehicles, and with respect to the implications for the operation of this Agreement of new automotive producers becoming established in Canada.

(c) No later than January 1, 1968, the two Governments shall jointly undertake a comprehensive review of the progress made towards achieving the objectives set forth in Article I. During this review the Governments shall consider such further steps as may be necessary or desirable for the full achievement of these objectives.

Article V

Access to the United States and Canadian markets provided for under this Agreement may by agreement be accorded on similar terms to other countries.

Article VI

This Agreement shall enter into force provisionally on the date of signature and definitively on the date upon which notes are exchanged between the two Governments giving notice that appropriate action in their respective legislatures has been completed.

Article VII

This Agreement shall be of unlimited duration. Each Government shall however have the right to terminate this Agreement twelve months from the date on which that Government gives written notice to the other Government of its intention to terminate the Agreement.

In witness whereof the representatives of the two Governments have signed this Agreement.

Done in duplicate at Johnson City, Texas, this 16th day of January 1965, in English and French, the two texts being equally authentic.

For the Government of the United States of America:

For the Government of Canada:

Annex A

1. (1) Automobiles; when imported by a manufacturer of automobiles.

   (2) All parts, and accessories and parts thereof, except tires and tubes, when imported for use as original equipment in automobiles to be produced in Canada by a manufacturer of automobiles.

   (3) Buses, when imported by a manufacturer of buses.

(4) All parts, and accessories and parts thereof, except tires and tubes, when imported for use as original equipment in buses to be produced in Canada by a manufacturer of buses.

(5) Specified commercial vehicles, when imported by a manufacturer of specified commercial vehicles.

(6) All parts, and accessories and parts thereof, except tires, tubes and any machines or other articles required under Canadian tariff item 438a to be valued separately under the tariff items regularly applicable thereto, when imported for use as original equipment in specified commercial vehicles to be produced in Canada by a manufacturer of specified commercial vehicles.

2. (1) "Automobile" means a four-wheeled passenger automobile having a seating capacity for not more than ten persons;

(2) "Base year" means the period of twelve months commencing on the 1st day of August, 1963 and ending on the 31st day of July, 1964;

(3) "Bus" means a passenger motor vehicle having a seating capacity for more than 10 persons, or a chassis therefor, but does not include any following vehicle or chassis therefor, namely an electric trackless trolley bus, amphibious vehicle, tracked or half-tracked vehicle or motor vehicle designed primarily for off-highway use;

(4) "Canadian value added" has the meaning assigned by regulations made under section 273 of the Canadian Customs Act;

(5) "Manufacturer" of vehicles of any following class, namely automobiles, buses or specified commercial vehicles, means, in relation to any importation of goods in respect of which the description is relevant, a manufacturer that

(i) produced vehicles of that class in Canada in each of the four consecutive three months' periods in the base year, and

(ii) produced vehicles of that class in Canada in the period of twelve months ending on the 31st day of July in which the importation is made,

(A) the ratio of the net sales value of which to the net sales value of all vehicles of that class sold for consumption in Canada by the manufacturer in that period is equal to or higher than the ratio of the net sales value of all vehicles of that class produced in Canada by the manufacturer in the base year to the net sales value of all vehicles of that class sold for consumption in Canada by the manufacturer in the base year, and is not in any case lower than seventy-five to one hundred; and

(B) the Canadian value added of which is equal to or greater than the Canadian value added of all vehicles of that class produced in Canada by the manufacturer in the base year;

(6) "Net sales value" has the meaning assigned by regulations made under section 273 of the Canadian Customs Act; and

(7) "Specified commercial vehicle" means a motor truck, motor truck chassis, ambulance or chassis therefor, or hearse or chassis therefor, but does not include:

(a) any following vehicle or a chassis designed primarily therefor, namely a bus, electric trackless trolley bus, amphibious vehicle, tracked or half-tracked vehicle, golf or invalid cart, straddle carrier, motor vehicle designed primarily for off-highway use, or motor vehicle specially constructed and equipped to perform special services or functions, such as, but not limited to, a fire engine, mobile crane, wrecker, concrete mixer or mobile clinic, or

(b) any machine or other article required under Canadian tariff item 438a to be valued separately under the tariff item regularly applicable thereto.

3. The Government of Canada may designate a manufacturer not falling within the categories set out above as being entitled to the benefit of duty-free treatment in respect of the goods described in this annex.

Annex B

(1) Motor vehicles for the transport of persons or articles as provided for in items 692.05 and 692.10 of the Tariff Schedules of the United States and chassis therefor, but not including electric trolley buses, three-wheeled vehicles, or trailers accompanying truck tractors, or chassis therefor.

(2) Fabricated components, not including trailers, tires, or tubes for tires, for use as original equipment in the manufacture of motor vehicles of the kinds described in paragraph (1) above.

(3) Articles of the kinds described in paragraphs (1) and (2) above include such articles whether finished or unfinished but do not include any article produced with the use of materials imported into Canada which

are products of any foreign country (except materials produced within the customs territory of the United States), if the aggregate value of such imported materials when landed at the Canadian port of entry, exclusive of any landing cost and Canadian duty, was —

(a) with regard to articles of the kinds described in paragraph (1), not including chassis, more than 60 percent until January 1, 1968, and thereafter more than 50 percent of the appraised customs value of the article imported into the customs territory of the United States; and

(b) with regard to chassis of the kinds described in paragraph (1), and articles of the kinds described in paragraph (2), more than 50 percent of the appraised customs value of the article imported into the customs territory of the United States.

Appendix B

Sample "Letter of Undertaking"[1]

Chrysler Canada Ltd.
Windsor, Ontario, January 13, 1965.

Hon. C. M. Drury,
Minister of Industry,
Ottawa, Canada

Dear Mr. Minister: I am writing with respect to the agreement between the Governments of Canada and the United States concerning production and trade in automotive products.

Chrysler Canada, Ltd. welcomes the agreement and supports its objectives. In this regard, our company notes that the Governments of Canada and the United States have agreed "* * * that any expansion of trade can best be achieved through the reduction or elimination of tariff and all other barriers to trade operating to impede or distort the full and efficient development of each country's trade and industrial potential ***." In addition, we note that the Governments of Canada and the United States "* * * shall seek the early achievement of the following objectives:

(a) The creation of a broader market for automotive products within which the full benefits of specialization and large-scale production can be achieved;

(b) The liberalization of United States and Canadian automotive trade in respect of tariff barriers and other factors tending to impede it, with a view to enabling the industries of both countries to participate on a fair and equitable basis in the expanding total market of the two countries;

(c) The development of conditions in which market forces may operate effectively to attain the most economic pattern of investment, production, and trade."

---

[1]Source: House Committee on Ways and Means, *Hearings on H.R. 6960, United States-Canada Automotive Products Agreement,* 89th Congress, 1st Session, 1965, pp. 158-59.

145

Our company also notes that the right to import motor vehicles and original equipment parts into Canada under the agreement is available to motor manufacturers in Canada who meet the conditions stipulated in the Motor Vehicles Tariff Order 1965.

These conditions are, in brief, that vehicle manufacturers shall maintain in each model year their domestic production of motor vehicles in the same ratio to their domestic sales of motor vehicles and the same dollar value of Canadian value added in the production of motor vehicles in Canada, as in the period August 1, 1963, to July 31, 1964.

In addition to meeting these stipulated conditions and in order to contribute to meeting the objectives of the agreement, Chrysler Canada Ltd. undertakes:

1. To increase in each model year over the preceding model year, the dollar value of Canadian value added in the production of vehicles and original equipment parts by an amount equal to 60 percent of the growth in the market for automobiles sold by our company for consumption in Canada and by an amount equal to 50 percent of the growth in the market for the commercial vehicles specified in tariff item 950 sold by our company for consumption in Canada, it being understood that in the event of a decline in the market a decrease in such dollar value of Canadian value added in the above percentages is acceptable. For this purpose, growth or decline in the market shall be measured as the difference between the cost to our company of vehicles sold in Canada during the current model year and the cost to our company of. vehicles sold in Canada during the preceding model year net of Federal sales taxes in both cases, and

2. To increase the dollar value of Canadian value added in the production of vehicles and original equipment parts over and above the amount that we achieved in the period August 1, 1963 to July 31, 1964 and that which we undertake to achieve in (1) above, by an amount of $33 million during the period August 1, 1967 to July 31, 1968.

Chrysler Canada Ltd. also agrees to report to the Minister of Industry, every 3 months beginning April 1, 1965, such information as the Minister of Industry requires pertaining to progress achieved by our company, as well as plans to fulfill our obligations under this letter. In addition, Chrysler Canada Ltd. understands that the Government will conduct an audit each year with respect to the matters described in this letter.

I understand that before the end of model year 1968 we will need to discuss together the prospects for the Canadian automotive industry and our company's program.

Yours sincerely,

Ron W. Todgham.

Appendix C

Technical Note to Chapter 2

In Section C of Chapter 2 an attempt is made to compare the efficiency of automotive production in Canada and the United States during 1963. The method used is to examine the burdens that arise from inefficiency: higher prices for automotive products and lower returns to factors employed in making these products. Some estimate of the comparative return on capital employed (r) is essential for this exercise. Prices might be higher and wage rates lower in Canada, not because of comparative inefficiency but because firms extracted a higher return on capital in their Canadian operations. The purpose of this note is to explore this possibility.

It is impossible to obtain comparable rates of return on capital directly from public information. Therefore, an indirect approach was adopted. From Table 6 we note that in 1963 the amount left over for payments to capital, after all expenses were deducted from sales, was only 63 percent as high in Canada as in the United States on a per-production-worker basis (VA — Wages and Salaries/Prod. Emp.: column 6).[1] Thus,

1) $(\frac{Kr}{PW})$ Can./$(\frac{Kr}{PW})$ U.S. $= 0.63,$

where $K =$ value of the capital stock expressed in U.S. dollars
$r =$ rate of return on capital
$PW =$ number of production workers

Although we cannot observe r directly, we can infer the ratio $r_{Can.}/r_{U.S.}$ if we can estimate $(\frac{K}{PW})$ Can./$(\frac{K}{PW})$ U.S.

The ratio K/PW is simply the capital-labour ratio. On *a priori* grounds it would seem that the capital-labour ratio should have been lower in the Canadian than in the U.S. automotive industry for two reasons.

---

[1]Since profits taxes are roughly the same in both countries, the difference between pre- and post-tax earnings is not distinguished here.

149

First, labour was relatively cheaper in Canada, so the Canadian manu-facturer should have been operating on the more labour-intensive portion of his production function. Second, Canada's tariff structure encouraged an automotive products mix concentrated on assembly and smaller parts, and this mix is considered to be less capital-intensive than for the total mix as produced in the United States. The key question for our purposes, however, is how much lower the capital-labour ratio was in Canada.

The procedure for estimating the relative capital-labour ratios is as follows. *First,* from Table 5 we observe that the automotive products output-labour ratio in Canada was 68 percent the level in the United States (VS/Emp.: column 1),[2] or

$$2) \ (\frac{VS}{PW}) \ \text{Can.}/(\frac{VS}{PW}) \ \text{U.S.} = 0.68$$

Second, the Wonnacotts have estimated that the capital-output ratio in the transportation equipment industry of Canada was 88 percent the level in the United States as of 1958.[3] We assume, for lack of a better alter-native, that this same relationship was observed in the automotive products segment in 1963. (Automotive products represented about 70 percent of total Canadian transportation equipment sales in 1963.) Thus, our assump-tion is that

$$3) \ (\frac{K}{VS}) \ \text{Can.}/(\frac{K}{VS}) \ \text{U.S.} = 0.88$$

Multiplying equation (2) by equation (3), we obtain

$$4) \ (\frac{K}{PW}) \ \text{Can.}/(\frac{K}{PW}) \ \text{U.S.} = 0.68 \times 0.88 = 0.60$$

In other words, our estimate is that the Canadian capital-labour ratio was equal to 60 percent the U.S. level in the automotive products industry as of 1963. Third, plugging this result back into equation (1), we get

$$5) \ 0.60 \ (r_{Can.}/r_{U.S.}) = 0.63, \text{ or } r_{Can.}/r_{U.S.} = 1.05.$$

Therefore, our estimate is that the rate of return on capital in Canada was slightly higher, by about 5 percent, than in the United States.

There are a number of shortcomings in this analysis, as there are in all efforts at indirect reasoning. Therefore, we should not place undue stress on the illusion of exactness in the above exercise, particularly in

---

[2]This merely restates the fact that the labour-output ratio was higher in Canada.
[3]*Free Trade Between the United States and Canada, op. cit.,* p. 183. Of seventeen industry categories reported, only three showed a lower capital-output ratio in Canada. The others were tobacco and petroleum products. For all manufacturing, the capital-output ratio was 15 percent higher in Canada.

the case of individual companies. What seems warranted is the conclusion that the average rates of return in the two countries were in the same general range. Any bias tending to overstate the rate of return in Canada adds another layer to the burdens of inefficiency in Canadian automotive production. A bias in the direction of understating the return in Canada would soften the conclusion of inefficiency arrived at on the basis of observations of 10 percent higher product prices and 30 percent lower wages.[4]

Finally, since the possibility of understating the relative rate of return in Canada is of some significance to our study, a further rough check has been attempted. Data filed under Canada's Corporations and Labour Unions Returns Act (CALURA) report fifty-five Canadian manufacturers of motor vehicles, parts, and accessories that were at least 50 percent foreign-owned. On average, these firms earned a return of 40.6 percent on equity, before tax, in 1963.[5] Halving this to reflect taxes yields about 20 percent. Among U.S. firms in the motor vehicle and equipment industry, the after-tax rate of return on net worth in 1963 was roughly 18 percent.[6] The difference would not appear to be significant enough to cast serious doubt on our conclusion of general comparability for rates of return. Still, wide variations are possible within broad industry aggregates. Rates of return for the "Big Three" in the United States for 1963 were: General Motors, 23 percent; Chrysler, 19 percent; Ford, 13 percent.[7] At least as great a variability undoubtedly existed for Canadian subsidiaries of these firms.

---

[4]Suppose, for illustration, that our estimate of the capital-output ratio in Canada is too high and the true ratio is only 62 percent of the U.S. level. Reworking the above example using this figure, we obtain $r_{Can.}/r_{U.S.} = 1.50$. Payments to capital (VA − Salaries and wages/PW, Table 6, column 6) represent about 20 percent of the value of shipments in Canada (VS/Pay, Table 5, column 1). Therefore, if the rate of return was 50 percent higher in Canada, this would tend to produce a 10 percent higher price (0.5 times 0.2) in Canada. In this case we might be wrong to attribute the higher price to lower Canadian efficiency.
[5]*Corporations and Labour Unions Returns Act, Report for 1963*, Part 1 (Ottawa: Department of Trade and Commerce, 1967), p. 67. These 55 firms accounted for Can.$1,965 million of total sales of Can.$2,075 million by all firms classified in automotive industries.
[6]*FTC-SEC Quarterly Financial Reports for Manufacturing Corporations*, 2nd Quarter, 1964 (Washington).
[7]"The 500 Largest U.S. Industrial Corporations," *Fortune*, May 15, 1964. These returns are on a consolidated basis, reflecting the companies' worldwide operations.

Appendix D

Trade Flows in Vehicles by Body Style

This appendix provides detailed background for the discussion of vehicle trade contained in Section C.2.a of Chapter 6. Table 14 in that chapter is a summary of the three tables in this appendix, which show trade patterns for the major types of vehicles body styles. Table D-1 indicates the degree of market penetration achieved in Canada by vehicles imported from the United States; Table D-2 shows the distribution of made-in-Canada vehicles between domestic and export markets; Table D-3 computes the ratio of imports to exports.

Several of the producers have objected that this type of analysis lacks relevance. Their point, which is generally valid, is that specialization in this industry takes place by vehicle line (e.g., Ford Maverick, Dodge Polara, etc.), and not by body style. Unfortunately, trade data are not published by vehicle line; and while a rough approximation could be made, the task is very time-consuming and in any event would be rather aggregative for certain of the producers. Therefore, trade by body style has been analyzed instead.

There is no real problem in Tables D-1 and D-2, since they show how great the degree of integration has become without trying to explain why. Table D-3 is a different matter. The ratio between shipments of made-in-Canada vehicles for export to shipments of vehicles imported from the United States may be interpreted as a rough indicator of locational production preferences. This is a conclusion to which some producers have taken particular exception.

It is granted that the apparent preference for Canadian production in the aggregate and in broad vehicle classes — as shown by the high rate of exports relative to imports in Table D-3 — may reflect producers' reactions to the requirements in the Agreement and the letters of undertaking, rather than a Canadian locational advantage in the absence of all trade barriers. But if this effect plus the fact that specialization occurs by vehicle lines were the only considerations, the relationship between exports and imports should be fairly constant among body styles, with no persistent trends emerging over time.

153

Yet persistent trends do emerge in Table D-3, namely:

1) Convertibles have consistently been sourced in the United States.

2) Station wagons are produced in Canada to a point where exports are currently six times imports.

3) The heaviest truck categories tend to be sourced in the United States.

4) Medium-weight trucks have been sourced in Canada to a point where in 1968 exports were more than seventeen times as great as imports in the 14,001- to 19,500-pound categories.[1]

If the industry were to start from scratch on the basis of duty-free trade in North America, the results might be quite different. But given conditions during the life of the Agreement, it can be seen from Table D-3 that some definite preference patterns do exist and, interestingly, these patterns were apparent well before the Agreement took effect in 1965.

TABLE D-1

MARKET SHARE IN CANADA OF FACTORY SHIPMENTS IMPORTED
TO CANADA FROM THE UNITED STATES, BY BODY STYLE, 1960-68[a]
(percentages)

Body Style	Calendar Year								
	1960	1961	1962	1963	1964	1965	1966	1967	1968
Total, all vehicles	7.0	5.1	3.6	1.3	2.4	6.3	17.8	37.5	41.1
Total, all cars	7.9	4.8	4.0	1.4	2.7	6.7	19.2	40.5	43.4
Convertibles	30.5	22.3	13.2	3.2	8.0	12.1	30.5	55.6	69.5
Hard tops:									
Two-door	6.8	7.2	6.3	3.1	7.5	13.6	31.4	53.2	52.1
Four-door	12.4	13.8	14.0	8.4	6.9	6.1	20.9	49.0	47.6
Sedans:									
Two-door	3.0	2.9	2.0	0.1	0.1	3.4	10.2	34.1	44.6
Four-door	7.1	2.1	2.1	0.2	0.5	3.4	11.2	27.5	30.7
Station wagons	10.3	6.2	3.3	1.2	1.4	3.8	16.1	28.9	31.1
Total, all trucks[b]	2.7	6.5	1.2	0.4	0.4	4.0	11.2	24.2	30.4
6,000 lbs. and under	4.0	10.0	1.4	0.4	0.4	4.8	12.9	25.6	29.8
6,001 to 10,000 lbs.	1.7	0.8	0.7	0.5	0.2	0.5	1.8	13.6	20.5
10,001 to 14,000 lbs.	1.2	1.7	2.1	6.3	5.7	4.2	4.4	5.8	1.9
14,001 to 16,000 lbs.	1.0	19.0	0.9	0.3	0.2	0.3	2.1	10.4	10.7
16,001 to 19,500 lbs.	0.3	neg.	0.6	0.1	0.1	6.2	13.7	24.3	37.8
19,501 to 26,000 lbs.	0.9	0.7	0.6	0.1	0.2	3.0	9.8	22.4	38.5
26,001 to 33,000 lbs.	8.3	3.3	1.7	1.1	1.5	6.2	22.9	28.9	47.5
Over 33,000 lbs.	4.0	2.3	1.8	0.3	0.4	7.7	21.5	47.8	55.0
Buses or coaches	60.0	68.5	2.8	1.8	0.7	22.8	27.6	9.7	35.5

Neg. = Negligible, less than 0.1 percent.
[a]Total market equals shipments of imports from United States plus domestic shipments of made-in-Canada vehicles. Imports exclude direct imports by final purchaser.
[b]By gross vehicle weight.
Source: See Table D-3.

[1]The sudden jump in the ratio for trucks in the 10,001- to 14,000-pound class during 1968 was evidently due to a reclassification of previous production in the next higher weight class. This could have resulted from a change of very few pounds in the weight of a particular line.

TABLE D-2

Unit Shipments for Export as a Percentage of Total Unit Factory Shipments
of Made-in-Canada Vehicles, by Body Style, 1960-68
(percentages)

	Calendar Year								
Body Style	1960	1961	1962	1963	1964	1965	1966	1967	1968
Total, all vehicles	5.8	3.3	3.5	3.3	6.7	11.3	31.5	51.3	59.4
Total, all cars	5.7	2.9	3.3	3.0	6.7	10.4	28.3	49.8	58.0
Convertibles	2.8	1.0	0.7	0.8	1.9	1.8	2.2	27.2	23.3
Hard tops:									
Two-door	1.1	0.5	0.3	0.4	1.9	4.7	19.5	41.4	48.9
Four-door	8.3	7.0	7.5	8.1	9.8	13.4	32.8	65.8	69.7
Sedans:									
Two-door	0.4	0.1	0.1	0.2	`5.0	13.4	45.3	61.5	69.6
Four-door	7.8	3.5	4.7	4.2	8.6	12.7	26.9	43.5	52.7
Station wagons	4.5	2.8	1.1	1.7	8.0	9.6	40.9	67.8	73.6
Total, all trucks[a]	6.3	5.6	4.9	4.6	6.7	16.3	42.1	56.8	64.3
6,000 lbs. and under	6.6	6.9	4.7	5.7	6.9	14.6	39.2	55.1	61.6
6,001 to 10,000 lbs.	5.3	4.6	5.3	6.8	8.8	19.9	49.6	63.8	69.9
10,001 to 14,000 lbs.	neg.	neg.	neg.	nil	0.2	0.3	nil	0.4	43.7
14,001 to 16,000 lbs.	9.8	8.7	8.1	2.7	9.5	27.8	41.8	63.1	66.3
16,001 to 19,500 lbs.	16.7	14.8	21.6	5.2	27.6	70.2	88.5	90.4	91.6
19,501 to 26,000 lbs.	nil	neg.	0.4	0.4	2.2	7.0	14.1	36.9	59.5
26,001 to 33,000 lbs.	nil	2.6	neg.	neg.	0.8	2.5	7.3	22.5	45.3
Over 33,000 lbs.	nil	1.1	1.5	neg.	0.1	neg.	1.2	13.8	33.3
Buses or coaches	nil	nil	neg.	neg.	0.6	3.3	67.2	15.1	22.4

Nil = Zero.
Neg. = Negligible, less than 0.1 percent.

[a]By gros vehicle weight.

Source: See Table D-3.

TABLE D-3

RATIO OF UNIT EXPORT SHIPMENTS OF MADE-IN-CANADA VEHICLES
TO UNIT FACTORY SHIPMENTS OF VEHICLES IMPORTED TO CANADA
FROM THE UNITED STATES, BY BODY STYLE, 1960-68[a]

Body Style	Calendar Year								
	1960	1961	1962	1963	1964	1965	1966	1967	1968
Total, all vehicles	.82	.63	.98	2.64	2.97	1.89	2.12	1.75	2.10
Total, all cars	.72	.59	.80	2.19	2.55	1.60	1.67	1.46	1.80
Convertibles	.06	.03	.04	.24	.23	.13	.05	.30	.13
Hard tops:									
Two-door	.15	.07	.04	.14	.24	.32	.53	.62	.88
Four-door	.64	.47	.50	.96	1.46	2.37	1.84	2.00	2.53
Sedans:									
Two-door	.12	.03	.05	1.39	51.74	4.40	7.32	3.08	2.84
Four-door	1.11	1.67	2.25	17.76	19.81	4.11	2.91	2.03	2.51
Station wagons	.41	.44	.34	1.38	5.94	2.73	3.61	5.18	6.16
Total, all trucks[b]	2.45	.85	4.30	11.51	19.85	4.71	5.76	4.11	4.12
6,000 lbs. and under	1.68	.66	3.34	15.17	20.52	3.37	4.35	3.57	3.79
6,001 to 10,000 lbs.	3.31	5.81	7.54	14.39	52.63	45.80	53.85	11.13	8.99
10,001 to 14,000 lbs.	.05	.04	.04	nil	.04	.06	nil	.06	39.16
14,001 to 16,000 lbs.	10.90	.40	9.30	8.29	42.17	151.45	33.68	14.81	16.39
16,001 to 19,500 lbs.	65.24	602.00	44.45	42.60	310.67	35.82	48.41	29.30	17.90
19,501 to 26,000 lbs.	nil	.10	.61	2.53	12.39	2.41	1.51	2.03	2.35
26,001 to 33,000 lbs.	nil	.79	.05	.03	.51	.38	.26	.71	.92
Over 33,000 lbs.	nil	.46	.83	.25	.38	neg.	.05	.18	.41
Buses or coaches	nil	nil	.03	.05	.78	.12	5.38	1.65	.52

Nil = Zero.
Neg. = Negligible, less than .01.

[a]Imports exclude direct imports by final purchaser.
[b]By gross vehicle weight.

Source: Computed from Dominion Bureau of Statistics, Cat. No. 42-002, as quoted
in *Facts and Figures of the Automotive Industry* (Toronto: Motor Vehicle
Manufacturers' Association (Canada), various issues).

Appendix E

Problems in Calculating the U.S. Automotive Trade Balance with Canada Following the 1965 Agreement

A bilateral balance of trade can be calculated on the basis of either country's imports and exports, both countries' imports, or both countries' exports, with allowance being made for the rate of exchange. Even if the two countries collect and classify trade information in exactly the same way, a somewhat different balance is likely to emerge from each combination of statistics. But the size of the discrepancies in the case of U.S.-Canada automotive trade has become so great that it has been the cause of considerable controversy.

Table E-1 illustrates the extent of the differences.[1] On the basis of either U.S. or Canadian official trade statistics (sections I and II of the table), the total U.S. automotive surplus with Canada increased between 1964 and 1965, followed by continuous declines thereafter. On the basis of U.S. export and import statistics, however, the 1964 to 1968 decline was $737.5 million, while Canadian statistics indicate a decline of only $187.0 million.[2]

As it has reported on the operation of the Agreement, the U.S. Administration has tried to resolve these discrepancies by suggesting that the best method for computing changes in the trade balance is to use each country's import statistics. On this basis, shown in section III of Table E-1, the U.S. surplus declined by $419.4 million between 1964 and 1968[3]. The rationale for this suggestion is that a commodity with several possible uses will be imported duty-free as an "automotive product"

---

[1]Automotive trade as reported includes some products not covered by the Agreement, such as replacement parts and specialty vehicles, on which duties have to be paid. Of total U.S. automotive imports from Canada of $2,579.8 million in 1968, duties were paid on $61.4 million.

[2]Throughout this appendix all values will be expressed in U.S. dollar equivalents, using when necessary the conversion rate $1 Can. = $0.925 U.S.

[3]*Second Annual Report of the President to the Congress on the Operation of the Automotive Products Trade Act of 1965* (Washington: Government Printing Office, 1968), p. 19. Import figures reported in official Canadian statistics (section II) have been adjusted in the tabulation of this import-import balance to achieve comparability in product coverage.

TABLE E-1

ALTERNATIVE MEASURES OF THE U.S. AUTOMOTIVE TRADE BALANCE WITH CANADA, 1964-68
(million dollars U.S.)

Calendar Year	I. U.S. Statistics			II. Canadian Statistics			III. Both Countries' Imports			IV. Both Countries' Exports		
	U.S. Exports	U.S. Imports	Balance[a]	Canadian Imports[c] (U.S. Exports)	Canadian Exports (U.S. Imports)	Balance[a]	Canadian Imports[c] (U.S. Exports)	U.S. Imports	Balance[a]	U.S. Exports	Canadian Exports (U.S. Imports)	Balance[a]
Total Automotive Products												
1964	654.1	75.9	+578.2	658.7	89.7	+569.0	659.3	75.9	+583.4	654.1	89.7	+564.4
1965	860.0	247.0	+613.0	930.2	212.6	+717.6	929.4	247.0	+682.4	860.0	212.6	+647.4
1966	1,311.4	889.1	+422.3	1,381.1	779.5	+601.6	1,415.9	889.1	+526.8	1,311.4	779.5	+531.9
1967	1,801.2	1,562.0	+239.2	1,942.0	1,464.7	+477.3	2,001.1	1,562.0	+439.1	1,801.2	1,464.7	+336.5
1968[b]	2,420.5	2,579.8	−159.3	2,641.8	2,259.8	+382.0	2,743.8	2,579.8	+164.0	2,420.5	2,259.8	+160.7
Passenger Cars												
1964	45.4	21.9	+23.5	41.1	19.3	+21.8	41.00	21.9	+19.1	45.4	19.3	+26.1
1965	114.0	84.1	+29.9	116.3	61.4	+54.9	116.0	84.1	+31.9	114.0	61.4	+52.6
1966	275.6	370.7	−95.1	291.8	322.1	−30.3	291.8	370.7	−78.9	275.6	322.1	−46.5
1967	563.0	818.0	−255.0	607.8	760.3	−152.5	613.0	818.0	−205.0	563.0	760.3	−197.3
1968[b]	703.6	1,348.9	−645.3	829.5	1,174.5	−345.0	831.8	1,348.9	−517.1	703.6	1,174.5	−470.9
Trucks, Buses, and Chassis												
1964	17.7	4.7	+13.0	21.2	4.7	+16.5	21.2	4.7	+16.5	17.7	4.7	+13.0
1965	45.4	23.7	+21.7	41.8	20.4	+21.4	41.7	23.7	+18.0	45.4	20.4	+25.0
1966	83.6	158.3	−74.7	86.2	135.3	−49.1	86.1	158.3	−72.2	83.6	135.3	+51.7
1967	138.3	269.9	−131.6	133.8	268.7	−134.9	133.8	269.9	−136.1	138.3	268.7	−130.4
1968[b]	166.6	447.9	−281.3	181.4	399.0	−217.6	196.0	447.9	−251.9	166.6	399.0	−232.4

TABLE E-1 (continued)

Parts and Accessories

1964	591.1	49.3	+541.8	65.7	596.4	+530.7	597.1	49.3	+547.8	591.1	65.7	+525.4
1965	700.5	139.2	+561.3	130.8	772.1	+641.3	771.7	139.2	+632.5	700.5	130.8	+569.7
1966	952.1	360.2	+591.9	322.1	1,003.1	+681.0	1,037.9	360.2	+677.7	952.1	322.1	+630.0
1967	1,099.9	474.1	+625.8	435.8	1,200.5	+764.7	1,254.3	474.1	+780.2	1,099.9	435.8	+664.1
1968^b	1,550.3	783.0	+767.3	686.3	1,630.9	+944.6	1,716.0	783.0	+933.0	1,550.3	686.3	+864.0

aImplied U.S. surplus (+) or deficit (−). bPreliminary and subject to revision. cThe discrepancies in these two sets of figures are due to differences in the products included. The import-import measure (section III) is reported on as consistent a basis as can be achieved in terms of product coverage.

Sources: For I. U.S. Statistics: *Third Annual Report of the President to the Congress on the Operation of the Automotive Products Trade Act of 1965* (Washington: Government Printing Office, 1969) p. 21. Also *Second Annual Report . . .;* 1968, p. 51; for II. Canadian Statistics: *Ibid.,* p. 25 and p. 57, respectively; for III. Both Countries' Imports: *Ibid.,* p. 10; for IV. Both Countries' Exports: derived from I and II.

under the Agreement only if it is specifically destined for inclusion in new vehicles. This means that data on automotive products imports provide an accurate and comprehensive record of automotive trade. The exporting country, however, has no real need to determine the precise end-use of the product and may not classify it in the automotive category. The U.S. Administration is, in effect, arguing that a significant amount of trade under the Agreement has been in products which, prior to the Agreement, would have been classified as non-automotive imports and still are classed as non-automotive in export statistics.

A. Discrepancies for Parts

The argument for using an import-import basis for calculating the trade balance makes a good deal of sense in the case of parts and accessories. Some parts can be used for a number of purposes and are reported as automotive products only when so declared by the importer. Sections I and II of Table E-1 show that U.S. exports of parts to Canada were reported to be $1,550 million in 1968, but that same year Canadian statistics report $1,631 million in parts imports from the United States. Using both countries' import figures (section III), adjusted for differences in product coverage, we obtain a U.S. surplus on parts trade in 1968 of $933 million, compared with $767 million reported in the U.S. statistics, a difference of $166 million in favour of the United States.

B. Discrepancies for Vehicles

The same argument in favour of import-import usage is meaningless in the case of most motor vehicles. There could hardly be any doubt as to whether a car or truck should be classified as an automotive product. Yet in 1968 U.S. exports of cars to Canada were valued at $704 million by the United States, while Canadian imports of cars from the United States were valued at $830 million. U.S. car imports from Canada, on the other hand, were valued at $1,349 million by the United States, while Canada valued its car exports at $1,174 million. There are three possible explanations for different estimates of vehicle trade, and this complicates the problem of getting an accurate reading.

1. Transportation Charges

One of the tricky problems in valuing trade between Canada and the United States involves the treatment of inland freight charges. Overseas trade is fairly easy to handle — as long as countries use the same method of valuation (f.o.b., c.i.f., etc.) — since goods are physically transferred at both the port of exit and the port of entry. Overland trade, particularly in the case of automotive products, usually requires no such transfer at the border, but rather the train or truck journey continues until an internal distribution centre is reached.

Valuation procedures in Canada generally exclude inland freight charges from the value of merchandise imports and exports. When such services are performed so that foreign-exchange payments or receipts are involved, entries are made in the transportation account of the balance of payments.[4] In the United States, customs regulations require that inland freight charges incurred in transferring imports to the foreign port of exit or exports to the U.S. port of exit be included in the valuation of merchandise trade.[5] In practice, however, it appears that trade with Canada has been valued exclusive of inland freight charges, probably because of the difficulty of breaking out that portion of the total transport haul involved in getting to the U.S. border.[6]

Because of the understatement of inland freight charges in the United States and their exclusion from the merchandise account in Canada, it will not make much difference how we estimate the U.S. automotive trade balance so far as these charges are concerned. In fact, because we are mainly interested in using the trade statistics to measure changes in the distribution of automotive production only, it is best that transportation charges are generally separated in practice.

2. Timing of Trade Flows

Exports are usually registered when a good is shipped or even as early as when it is consigned for shipment to a foreign buyer. Imports, on the other hand, may not be registered until received or until payment is actually made. The lag between reporting a good as an export by one country and that same good as an import by another country may therefore be quite long. When trade is expanding as rapidly as has been the case in automotive products, this lag may cause considerable distortions between countries' trade statistics.

The solution to the timing problem is to use either an import-import or an export-export basis for evaluating changes in the U.S. trade balance. This method puts the statistics within the same timing framework, either on an as-shipped or on an as-received basis.

---

[4]For a discussion of freight and shipping in Canada's balance of payments, see John W. Popkin, *Non-Merchandise Transactions Between Canada and the United States* (Montreal and Washington: Canadian-American Committee, 1963), Chap. 7.
[5]See Report of the Review Committee for Balance of Payments Statistics to the Bureau of the Budget, *The Balance of Payments Statistics of the United States: A Review and Appraisal* (Washington: Government Printing Office, 1965) pp. 40-42.
[6]U.S. Department of Commerce, Office of Business Economics, *Survey of Current Business*, June 1969, p. 44. In 1968, the total of all merchandise exports from the United States to Canada was adjusted upward by $228 million to reflect the understatement of inland freight.

3. Determining the Price for Traded Products

The final problem is the most difficult to explain, yet its clarification plays a fundamental role in reconciling the discrepancies in trade data for vehicles. It arises from the uncertainty about how to value goods exchanged under the Agreement when virtually all vehicle trade and much of the parts trade between Canada and the United States represents intracompany transfers. With vehicle prices still being higher in Canada than in the United States, the choice of the right price for products moving between the two countries is not an obvious one.

The best explanation for the discrepancies in the figures on trade in completed vehicles that we have heard is as follows:[7]

• First, U.S. imports are valued on the basis of wholesale market (dealers') prices in Canada, in accordance with U.S. customs regulations regarding "dumping" (selling the same good in a foreign market at a lower price than in the home market).

• Second, for somewhat similar reasons, Canadian imports are valued at the wholesale market (dealers') price in the United States.

• Third, both countries' export statistics are based on intracompany transfer prices established by the firms themselves. It is claimed that there is only one transfer price for each vehicle, and this price is below the dealers' price in both countries.

If we accept the validity of these propositions, which of the possible measures of the net trade balance is most meaningful?

The least acceptable bases for measurement are the balances calculated from either country's export-import figures. With exports valued at transactions prices and imports valued at dealers' prices, there is no consistent basis for comparison.

Analyses based upon import-import statistics are also invalid, but for very different reasons. Because of differentials in vehicle prices in the two countries, companies may earn higher profits on sales of U.S. vehicles in Canada than on sales of Canadian vehicles in the United States. If imports were valued at dealers' prices in the *importing* country, we might want to use the import-import basis to incorporate this factor of different profit margins. Imports are supposedly valued at dealers' prices in the *exporting* country, however, so we doubt that there is any rationale at all for using a balance computed on the import-import basis in the case of completed vehicles.

---

[7]This explanation came from discussions with the Office of Business Economics, U.S. Department of Commerce.

We are left, then, with an export-export basis when pricing and valuation problems of the kind encountered in vehicle trade arise. This method, based upon common prices for trade in either direction, is the only one available that allows us to achieve meaningful consistency.[8]

Table E-2 summarizes this discussion of the effects of valuation procedures. As is shown there, an exchange of two identical vehicles would lead to a decrease in the reported U.S. trade balance on a U.S. export-import or an import-import basis of measurement, and a decline on a Canadian export-import basis of measurement. The export-export measure shows no change, which is the only meaningful result for this transaction.

C. Suggestion for "Best Estimate"

In summary, we have described in this appendix the reasons why changes in the U.S. automotive trade balance with Canada since the Agreement are not adequately measured on the basis of either country's exports and imports or even both countries' imports, as has been officially suggested in the U.S. Taking all factors into account as best we can from public information, our recommendation is to use the following hybrid measure:

• In the case of parts trade, valuation problems do exist, but the dominant reason for statistical discrepancies is inconsistency in product classification between imports and exports. An import-import basis (section III, Table E-1) is suggested to overcome this difficulty.

• With vehicle trade some differences in product classifications may possibly exist, but the valuation problem predominates. An export-export basis (section IV, Table E-1) is recommended for measuring the trade balance of these products. Combining these two measures (import-import for parts and export-export for vehicles) produces our "best estimate" of the over-all U.S. automotive trade balance with Canada, as presented in Table 19 of the main text, and in Chart 5. Comparisons of our "best estimate" measure with the other alternatives are shown in Table E-3.

One final point should be mentioned here. The four main vehicle-producers have supplied the U.S. government with estimates of their "balance of trade" in Canadian and United States operations between

---

[8]The June, 1969, *Survey of Current Business (op. cit.,* p. 44) seems to be trying to achieve the same result by adjusting U.S. imports downward by $300 million in 1968 to reflect the overstatement of vehicle imports from Canada. We do not understand how this amount was determined, however, since the difference between U.S. vehicle imports and Canadian vehicle exports was only $223 million that year (from Table E-1).

TABLE E-2

EXAMPLE OF THE EFFECTS OF DIFFERENCES IN VALUATION
PROCEDURES ON ESTIMATES OF THE VEHICLE TRADE BALANCE

Part A: Valuation of a Particular Vehicle in Trade Statistics

Line	Trade Account	Basis of Valuation	Hypothetical Value
1	U.S. exports	Intracompany transfer price	$2,000
2	U.S. imports	Canadian dealers' price	$2,200
3	Canadian exports	Intracompany transfer price	$2,000
4	Canadian imports	U.S. dealers' price	$2,100

Part B: Calculated Effect on the U.S. Trade Balance from an Exchange of Two
Identical Vehicles

Line	Measure of U.S. Balance	Calculation (From Part A above)	Reported Effect in U.S. Balance
5	U.S. export-import	Line 1 minus Line 2	−$200
6	Canadian export-import	Line 4 minus Line 3	+$100
7	Both countries' imports	Line 4 minus Line 2	−$100
8	Both countries' exports	Line 1 minus Line 3	0

TABLE E-3

COMPARATIVE MEASURES OF THE U.S. BALANCE OF AUTOMOTIVE TRADE
(million dollars U.S.)

Method of Measurement	1964	1968	Change: 1964 to 1968
U.S. import and export data	+578.2	−159.3	−737.5
Canadian import and export data	+569.0	+382.0	−187.0
Both countries' import data	+583.4	+164.0	−419.4
Both countries' export data	+564.4	+160.7	−393.7
"Best estimate": each country's import data for parts; export data for vehicles	+586.3	+229.7	−356.6

Source: Table E-1 and Table 19.

1966 and 1968.[9] In the aggregate these estimates show a decline of only $140.2 million in the U.S. trade surplus in this period, compared with $349.8 million on the basis of our estimates (from Table E-3). Unfortunately, only the barest of details have been made available by the U.S. government, and until independent researchers are given the opportunity to examine precise breakdowns of the data and to evaluate the nature of the assumptions upon which they are based, these estimates are of little practical value.[10]

---

[9]The results were (mil. $ U.S.)

	1966	1967	1968
U.S. sales to Canada	1,235.3	1,734.9	2,342.5
U.S. purchases from Canada	744.1	1,280.6	1,991.5
Implied balance (U.S. surplus)	491.2	454.3	351.0

Source: Third Annual Report of the President..., op. cit., p. 11.

[10]As one result of a meeting between the U.S. and Canadian governments in November, 1969, a subcommittee was established to investigate the problems associated with trade and production statistics in the two countries. The results of this investigation were not available at the time this study was completed.

Appendix F

Growth in the Factory Cost of Vehicle Sales
in Canada, 1964-68

The letters of undertaking with the Canadian government committed vehicle-manufacturers in Canada to an expansion of Canadian production (value added) as their vehicle sales in Canada increased. To determine the dollar value of this commitment, the growth in the factory cost of vehicles sold in Canada is to be multiplied by 0.6 for passenger cars and 0.5 for trucks and buses. There are no publicly available statistics on the factory cost of Canadian vehicle sales, so in order to carry on an analysis of the impact of this growth commitment, an estimating procedure had to be found. Table F-1 describes the method we have adopted.

Figures on sales of North American-produced vehicles in Canada, in units, are available from the Dominion Bureau of Statistics (Cat. No. 63-007), as shown in lines 3 and 6 of Table F-1. Vehicle imports from the United States are provided by the same source (in Cat. No. 65-007), in terms of both units and values (lines 1 and 4). Subtracting imports (lines 1 and 4) from total sales in Canada (lines 3 and 6), we obtain an estimate of the number of Canadian-produced vehicles sold in Canada (lines 2 and 5). What remains is to estimate the factory cost of vehicles produced and sold in Canada.

In 1964 a total of 558,210 cars having a wholesale value of Can.$1,561 million were shipped from Canadian plants, along with 112,096 trucks and buses having a wholesale value of Can.$296 million (DBS, Cat. No. 42-209). Dividing units shipped into the aggregate wholesale value, which is roughly equal to factory cost, we estimate that the factory cost was about Can.$2,210 per car and Can.$2,640 per truck and bus in 1964. Multiplying these amounts by the number of unit sales yields the total factory cost of vehicles produced and sold in Canada (line 2). This estimate is added to the value of imports (line 1) to give us the factory cost of all Canadian vehicle sales in 1964.

Wholesale values for Canadian vehicle shipments in 1968 were not available at the time this study was being completed. Furthermore, estimates for 1965 through 1967 suggest that distortions might arise in

165

attempting to carry this method forward. There appears to have been, for example, a shift in the production mix in Canada as a result of the Agreement, with greater concentration upon production of lower-cost vehicles for export markets, particularly in the case of trucks and buses.[1]

TABLE F-1

ESTIMATED FACTORY COST OF VEHICLE SALES IN CANADA,
CALENDAR YEARS 1964 AND 1968

Line		Cars		Commercial Vehicles	
		Number	Value	Number	Value
				(mil. $ Can.)	
	1964				
1	Imports[a]	15,138	44.3	3,331	22.9
2	Produced domestically	535,685	1,183.8	103,423	272.0
3	Total sales[b]	550,823	1,228.1	106,754	294.9
	1968				
4	Imports[a]	308,359	896.7	57,277	195.8
5	Produced domestically	328,885	726.8	84,925	224.2
6	Total sales[b]	637,244	1,623.5	142,202	420.0
7	Increase in value between 1964 and 1968 (line 6 minus line 3)		395.4		125.1
	In U.S. dollars ($1 Can. = $0.925 U.S.)		365.6		115.7

[a]Imports from the United States only.

[b]Sales of North American-produced vehicles only.

Sources: Dominion Bureau of Statistics, Cat. Nos. 65-007, 63-007, and 42-209, as quoted in *Facts and Figures of the Automotive Industry* (Toronto: Motor Vehicle Manufacturers' Association (Canada), various issues).

Because of the difficulty in obtaining data for per unit factory costs of domestic production in 1968, the estimates for 1964 are used again in 1968. The primary justification for this assumption is that indices of industry selling prices for Canadian vehicle sales were roughly the same

---

[1]Per unit wholesale values of Candian vehicle shipments have been as follows:

Calendar Year	Cars	Trucks and Buses
1964	C$2,210	C$2,640
1965	2,210	2,520
1966	2,120	2,230
1967	2,270	2,260

Source: Dominion Bureau of Statistics, Cat. No. 42-209. Some portion of the decline prior to 1967 may have been due to reductions in production costs following the Agreement, although we cannot estimate the amount, and this would mean that our estimates of sales growth are biased upward. See, however, the following footnote.

in 1968 as in 1964.[2] The calculation of the values shown in lines 5 and 6 of Table F-1, then, follows that for lines 2 and 3. Comparing lines 3 and 6, we estimate that the factory cost of Canadian car sales increased by Can.$395.4 million (U.S.$365.6 million) between 1964 and 1968, while for trucks and buses the increase was Can.$125.1 million (U.S.$115.7 million) (line 7).

Because of the questionable nature of our assumption about factory costs in 1968, it is useful to discuss the sensitivity of our results to changes in this assumption. Suppose, for example, that per unit costs were Can.$100 lower than our estimate. This would mean that the growth in the value of factory costs (line 7) would be Can.$32.9 million lower for cars and Can.$8.5 million lower for trucks and buses (from multiplying the units in line 5 by minus $100). The potential growth of U.S. exports as a result of increased Canadian sales (see Table 21) would then be Can.$17.4 million lower [(0.4) (C$32.9) + (0.5) (C$8.5)].

What this means is that we would be able to miss the true value of per unit factory costs by Can.$100 and still end up with a difference of only U.S.$16.1 million (0.925 times Can. $17.4 million) in our estimate of the extent to which the vehicle-manufacturers have exceeded their value-added growth commitments (Table 21). Since our estimate of this excess is U.S.$396 million, we can see that it is not very sensitive to errors in the assumption about per unit factory costs.

---

[2]The indices have performed as follows:

Calendar Year	Cars	Trucks
1964	100.0	100.0
1965	98.9	99.3
1966	97.9	99.7
1967	98.2	99.4
1968	100.2	102.2

Source: *Third Annual Report of the President to the Congress on the Operation of the Automotive Products Trade Act of 1965* (Washington: Government Printing Office, 1968), p. 16. The dip in the index for cars through 1966 conforms with the results in footnote 1 above, suggesting the possibility of a decline in the absolute cost of Canadian car production in this period. The performance for trucks, however, suggests a greater likelihood of a change in product mix as the factor explaining the decline in per unit wholesale value noted above.

MEMBERS OF THE CANADIAN-AMERICAN COMMITTEE

Co-chairmen

ROBERT M. FOWLER
President, Canadian Pulp and Paper
Association, Montreal, Quebec

JOHN R. WHITE
Vice President and Director, Standard Oil
Company (New Jersey), New York, New York

Members

I. W. ABEL
President, United Steelworkers of America,
AFL-CIO, Pittsburgh, Pennsylvania

T. N. BEAUPRE
Chairman of the Board and President,
Domtar Limited, Montreal, Quebec

J. A. BEIRNE
President, Communications Workers of
America, AFL-CIO, Washington, D.C.

WILLIAM J. BENNETT
President, Iron Ore Company of Canada,
Montreal, Quebec

HAROLD BOESCHENSTEIN
Chairman, Executive Committee, Owens-Corning
Fiberglas Corp., Toledo, Ohio

PHILIP BRIGGS
Vice President, Metropolitan Life,
New York, New York

E. D. BROCKETT, JR.
Chairman of the Board, Gulf Oil Corporation,
Pittsburgh, Pennsylvania

ARDEN BURBIDGE
Park River, North Dakota

EARL L. BUTZ
Vice President for Special Projects,
Purdue Research Foundation, Lafayette, Indiana

FRANCOIS E. CLEYN
Chairman of the Board and Chief Executive
Officer, Cleyn & Tinker, Ltd.,
Huntingdon, Quebec

STEPHEN C. EYRE
Senior Vice President, First National
City Bank, New York, New York

THOMAS E. COVEL
Vice President, Aluminium Limited, Inc.,
New York, New York

PAUL DESMARAIS
Chairman, Power Corporation of Canada,
Limited, Montreal, Quebec

WILLIAM DODGE
Secretary-Treasurer, Canadian Labour Congress,
Ottawa, Ontario

A. D. DUNTON
President, Carleton University,
Ottawa, Ontario

H. E. EKBLOM
Senior Vice President, The Chase Manhattan
Bank, New York, New York

EDMUND H. FALLON
Executive Vice President and General Manager,
Agway Inc., Syracuse, New York

MARCEL FARIBAULT
Montreal, Quebec

A. J. FISHER
President, Fiberglas Canada Limited,
Toronto, Ontario

J. R. FLUOR
Chairman and Chief Executive Officer, Fluor
Corporation, Ltd., Los Angeles, California

HAROLD S. FOLEY
Vancouver, British Columbia

JOHN F. GALLAGHER
Vice President, International Operations, Sears,
Roebuck and Co., Chicago, Illinois

G. H. GALLAWAY •
President, Crown Zellerbach International,
Inc., San Francisco, California

WILLIAM E. GRACE
President, Fruehauf Corporation,
Detroit, Michigan

169

*JOHN A. HANNAH
Washington, D.C.

F. PEAVEY HEFFELFINGER
Honorary Chairman of the Board and Member
of the Executive Committee, Peavey Company,
Minneapolis, Minnesota

GILBERT W. HUMPHREY
Chairman, The Hanna Mining Company,
Cleveland, Ohio

CURTIS M. HUTCHINS
Chairman of the Board, Dead River Company,
Bangor, Maine

R. A. IRWIN
President, Consolidated-Bathurst Ltd.,
Montreal, Quebec

CRAWFORD T. JOHNSON
Assistant to the Chairman,
Baker Industries, New York, New York

VERNON E. JOHNSON
Calumet, Quebec

JOSEPH D. KEENAN
International Secretary, International
Brotherhood of Electrical Workers, AFL-CIO,
Washington, D.C.

DAVID KIRK
Executive Secretary, The Canadian Federation
of Agriculture, Ottawa, Ontario

WILLIAM LADYMAN
International Vice-President, International
Brotherhood of Electrical Workers,
AFL-CIO-CLC, Toronto, Ontario

HERBERT H. LANK
Director, Du Pont of Canada, Limited,
Montreal, Quebec

PAUL LEMAN
President, Aluminum Company of Canada,
Limited, Montreal, Quebec

FRANKLIN A. LINDSAY
President, Itek Corporation,
Lexington, Massachusetts

DONALD MacDONALD
President, Canadian Labour Congress,
Ottawa, Ontario

ROBERT P. MacFADDEN
Director, Farrell Lines, Inc.,
New York, New York

ROBERT M. MacINTOSH
Deputy Chief General Manager, The Bank
of Nova Scotia, Toronto, Ontario

M. W. MACKENZIE
Como, Quebec

W. A. MACKINTOSH
Kingston, Ontario

WILLIAM MAHONEY
National Director, United Steelworkers of
America, AFL-CIO-CLC, Toronto, Ontario

AUGUSTINE R. MARUSI
Chairman and President, Borden Inc.,
New York, New York

BROOKS McCORMICK
President, International Harvester Company,
Chicago, Illinois

RALPH T. McELVENNY
Chairman and Chief Executive Officer,
American Natural Gas Company,
Detroit, Michigan

N. FLOYD McGOWIN
Chapman, Alabama

JOSEPH MORRIS
Executive Vice President, Canadian Labour
Congress, Ottawa, Ontario

KENNETH D. NADEN
Executive Vice President, National Council
of Farmer Cooperatives, Washington, D.C.

THOMAS S. NICHOLS
Chairman of the Executive Committee,
Olin Mathieson Chemical Corporation,
New York, New York

JOSEPH E. NOLAN
Senior Vice President-Administration,
Weyerhaeuser Company, Tacoma, Washington

VICTOR deB. OLAND
Halifax, Nova Scotia

I. H. PECK
President, Canadian International Paper
Company, Montreal, Quebec

MARCEL PEPIN
National President, Confederation of National
Trade Unions, Montreal, Quebec

CHARLES PERRAULT
President, Conseil du Patronat du Québec,
Montreal, Quebec

*Did not participate in the action of the Committee on this publication.

R. E. POWELL
Honorary Chairman, Aluminum Company
of Canada, Limited, Montreal, Quebec

HERBERT V. PROCHNOW
Honorary Director, The First National Bank
of Chicago, Chicago, Illinois

JAY RODNEY REESE
Vice President, Texas Instruments
Incorporated, Dallas, Texas

CHARLES RITZ
Honorary Chairman of the Board, International
Milling Company, Inc., Minneapolis, Minnesota

HOWARD I. ROSS
Dean of the Faculty of Management,
McGill University, Montreal, Quebec

HENRY E. RUSSELL
President, Carling Brewing Company,
Cleveland, Ohio

THOMAS W. RUSSELL, JR.
Chairman, Abex Corporation,
New York, New York

CLAUDE RYAN
Publisher-Editor, *Le Devoir,*
Montreal, Quebec

KARL E. SCOTT
President, Ford Motor Company of Canada,
Limited, Oakville, Ontario

LEROY D. SMITHERS
President, Dow Chemical of Canada, Limited,
Sarnia, Ontario

H. CHRISTIAN SONNE
New York, New York

CLAUDE O. STEPHENS
Chairman of the Board, Texas Gulf Sulphur
Company, Incorporated, New York, New York

J. E. WALLACE STERLING
Chancellor, Stanford University,
Stanford, California

R. DOUGLAS STUART
Director, The Quaker Oats Company,
Chicago, Illinois

ROBERT D. STUART, JR.
President, The Quaker Oats Company,
Chicago, Illinois

JAMES SUFFRIDGE
International President Emeritus, Retail Clerks
International Association, AFL-CIO,
Washington, D.C.

HAROLD W. SWEATT
Honorary Chairman of the Board,
Honeywell Inc., Minneapolis, Minnesota

A. W. TARKINGTON
Vice Chairman of the Board, Continental Oil
Company, New York, New York

RICHARD F. TUCKER
Executive Vice President, Mobil Oil
Corporation, New York, New York

E. K. TURNER
President, Saskatchewan Wheat Pool,
Regina, Saskatchewan

WILLIAM I. M. TURNER, JR.
President, Power Corporation of Canada,
Limited, Montreal, Quebec

W. O. TWAITS
President, Imperial Oil Limited,
Toronto, Ontario

HENRY S. WINGATE
Chairman, The International Nickel Company
of Canada, Limited, New York, New York

FRANCIS G. WINSPEAR
Chartered Accountant and Company Director,
Edmonton, Alberta

DAVID J. WINTON
The Winton Company,
Minneapolis, Minnesota

ARNOLD S. ZANDER
Professor, University of Wisconsin,
Green Bay, Wisconsin

Member Emeritus

HON. N. A. M. MacKENZIE
Vancouver, British Columbia

SELECTED PUBLICATIONS
OF THE CANADIAN-AMERICAN COMMITTEE*

Commercial Relations

The Canada-U.S. Automotive Agreement: An Evaluation, by Carl E. Beigie. 1970 ($3.00)

U.S.-Canadian Free Trade: The Potential Impact on the Canadian Economy, by Paul Wonnacott and Ronald J. Wonnacott. 1968 ($1.50)

Constructive Alternatives to Proposals for U.S. Import Quotas, a Statement by the Committee. 1968 ($1.00)

A New Trade Strategy for Canada and the United States, a Statement by the Committee. 1966 ($1.00)

A Possible Plan for a Canada-U.S. Free Trade Area, a Staff Report. 1965 ($1.50)

A Canada-U.S. Free Trade Arrangement: Survey of Possible Characteristics, by Sperry Lea. 1963 ($2.00)

Invisible Trade Barriers Between Canada and the United States, by Francis Masson and H. Edward English. 1963 ($1.50)

Non-Merchandise Transactions Between Canada and the United States, by John W. Popkin. 1963 ($1.50)

Basic Commodities and Agriculture

North American Agriculture in a New World, by J. Price Gittinger. 1970 ($2.00)

The U.S. Softwood Lumber Situation in a Canadian-American Perspective,[1] by Sperry Lea. 1962 ($1.00)

Investment

The Performance of Foreign-Owned Firms in Canada, by A. E. Safarian. 1969 ($2.00)

Capital Flows Between Canada and the United States, by Irving Brecher. 1965 ($2.00)

Recent Canadian and U.S. Government Actions Affecting U.S. Investment in Canada[2], a Statement by the Committee and a Staff Report. 1964 ($1.00)

Policies and Practices of United States Subsidiaries in Canada, by John Lindeman and Donald Armstrong. 1961 ($2.00)

Law and United States Business in Canada, by Kingman Brewster, Jr. 1960 ($1.00)

---

*These publications may be ordered from the Committee's offices at 1606 New Hampshire Avenue, N.Y., Washington, D.C. 20009, and at 2060 Sun Life Building, Montreal 110, Quebec. Quantity discounts are given. A descriptive flyer of these publications is also available.

[1] Contains *The U.S. Lumber Assistance Program and Canadian-American Relations,* a Policy Statement by the Committee issued earlier in 1962 in mimeographed form.

[2] Contains *Preserving the Canada-U.S. Common Market for Capital,* a Policy Statement by the Committee issued in 1963 in mimeographed form.